GOVERNANCE REFORM

**Poverty Reduction and Economic Management
Vice Presidency, The World Bank**

GOVERNANCE REFORM

BRIDGING MONITORING AND ACTION

BRIAN LEVY

© 2007 The International Bank for Reconstruction and Development / The World Bank
1818 H Street NW
Washington DC 20433
Telephone: 202-473-1000
Internet: www.worldbank.org
E-mail: feedback@worldbank.org

Cover design: Chris Lester, Rock Creek Creative, Bethesda, Maryland.
Cover map: Map design unit of the World Bank, based on data provided by the staff of the Development Data Group of the World Bank's Development Economics Vice Presidency. Cover photo credits (left to right, from back cover to the front): Chilean woman, Curt Carnemark; Brazilian man, Scott Wallace; Latvian girl, Curt Carnemark; Uzbekistani man, Anatoliy Rakhimbayev; Turkish woman, Scott Wallace; Rwandan boy, Arne Hoel; Yemeni woman and Senegalese girl, Scott Wallace; Ethiopian boy, Arne Hoel; Moroccan woman and Yemeni man, Scott Wallace; Indian youth, John Isaac; Bangladeshi girl, Scott Wallace; Sri Lankan woman, Dominic Sansoni; Vietnamese woman and child, Tran Thi Hoa; Indonesian man, Curt Carnemark. Photos courtesy of World Bank Photo Library.

1 2 3 4 10 09 08 07

ISBN-10: 0-8213-7032-4
ISBN-13: 978-0-8213-7032-2
eISBN: 0-8213-7033-2
DOI: 10.1596/978-0-8213-7032-2

Library of Congress Cataloging-in-Publication Data

Levy, Brian, 1954–
 Governance reform : bridging monitoring and action / by Brian Levy.
     p. cm.
Includes bibliographical references and index.
ISBN-13: 978-0-8213-7032-2
ISBN-10: 0-8213-7032-4
ISBN-10: 0-8213-7033-2 (electronic)
 1. Public administration—Developing countries. 2. Developing countries—Politics and government. I. Title.
  JF60.L49 2007
  3523'67091724—dc22

                                                              2007002739

Contents

Boxes

Figures

Tables

Acronyms and Abbreviations

ACBF	Africa Capacity Building Foundation
ADF	Albanian Development Fund
AERC	African Economic Research Consortium
AfDB	African Development Bank
BEEPS	Business Environment and Enterprise Performance Survey
BIS	baseline indicator set
CDD	community-driven development
CEPEJ	European Commission for the Efficiency of Justice
CPIA	Country Policy and Institutional Assessment
CPRGS	Comprehensive Poverty Reduction and Growth Strategy
CS	civil service
CSO	civil society organization
DAC	Development Assistance Committee
DB	Doing Business
DEC	Development Economics
DFID	Department for International Development (UK)
DSBB	Dissemination Standards Bulletin Board
EA	executive agency
EITI	Extractive Industries' Transparency Initiative
EPZ	export processing zone
FOI	freedom of information
GDDS	General Data Dissemination System
GDP	gross domestic product
GII	Global Integrity index
GMR	*Global Monitoring Report*
HIPC	heavily indebted poor countries
IBRD	International Bank for Reconstruction and Development
ICS	Investment Climate Survey

IDA	International Development Association
IMF	International Monetary Fund
KDP	Kecamatan Development Program
KK	Kaufmann-Kraay
KKZ	Kaufmann, Kraay, and Zoido-Lobaton
MAPS	Marrakech Action Plan for Statistics
MDG	Millennium Development Goal
MIC	middle-income countries
MIMDES	Ministry of Women and Social Development
MTEF	medium-term expenditure framework
NGO	nongovernmental organization
NPM	new public management
NURC	National Unity and Reconciliation Commission
OAS	Organization of American States
OECD	Organisation for Economic Co-operation and Development
PEFA	Public Expenditure and Financial Accountability
PFM	public financial management
PREM	Poverty Reduction Economic Management
PRS	poverty reduction strategy
RoL	Rule of Law
ROSC	Report on the Observance of Standards and Codes
SDDS	Special Data Dissemination Standard
SEDP	Socio-Economic Development Plan
TI	Transparency International
TV	transparency and voice
UNDP	United Nations Development Programme
VA	voice and accountability
WB	World Bank
WDR	World Development Report

Acknowledgments

This occasional paper is an extended version of chapters 5 and 6 of the *Global Monitoring Report 2006: Millennium Development Goals, Strengthening Mutual Accountability: Aid, Trade and Governance*. The author, Brian Levy, is Advisor, Public Sector Governance in the Poverty Reduction Economic Management (PREM) Vice Presidency. Overall guidance for this paper was provided by Alan Gelb (Director, DEC), and Sanjay Pradhan (Director, PREM). Research support was provided by Ceren Ozer. Valuable contributions were provided by Mark Sundberg (who led preparation of the 2006 GMR), Jim Anderson, Robert Beschel, Christina Biebesheimer, Rob Chase, Rui Coutinho, Bill Dorotinsky, Janet Entwistle, Daniel Kaufmann, Phil Keefer, Steve Knack, Sahr Kpundeh, Aart Kraay, Danny Leipziger, Carlos Leite, Rick Messick, Anand Rajaram, Francesca Recanatini, Randi Ryterman, Gary Reid, Sachin Shahria, Rick Stapenhurst and Joel Turkewitz.

Foreword

Strong empirical evidence links better governance to poverty reduction. The causal relationship is two-way. Gains in per capita income can contribute to the strengthening of a middle class and to demands for better governance. And gains in governance can contribute to an acceleration of income growth by increasing predictability, lengthening the decision horizon for economic actors, and making growth more inclusive. Helping build capable and accountable states has thus become an increasingly important part of the array of World Bank efforts to help reduce global poverty.

The high priority of public sector governance work is evident in the work program of the Bank's Poverty Reduction Economic Management (PREM) Network. One overarching objective of PREM is to increase the effectiveness of the Bank's poverty reduction efforts at the country level. Our advice is based in part on analytical work and policy lessons showing how good government and institutional reforms undergird growth and poverty reduction. Understanding better the relationships between governance and poverty reduction, giving better policy advice on governance reform, and helping design and implement better ways to monitor trends in governance at the country level are all frontier challenges for PREM.

This book is an extension of the framework and approach to governance and its monitoring prepared jointly by PREM and the World Bank's Development Economics Group, and presented in the 2006 Global Monitoring Report, *Strengthening Mutual Accountability*. The book lays out a framework for analyzing and monitoring governance, and applies it to low-income countries. It examines options for monitoring and reform of each of the components of a governance system, and it shows how different country-specific institutional starting points lead to different trajectories of governance reform. It explores how efforts to strengthen governance on the one hand, and improve service provision and the investment climate on the other, can be mutually reinforcing. We hope that the book will contribute to the important governance work of the Bank and that it will help inform a wider audience of concerned citizenry.

Danny Leipziger
Vice President
Poverty Reduction Economic Management Network
The World Bank

Preface

Building capable and accountable states is key to reducing poverty. Effective efforts to combat corruption are key to addressing the fiduciary and reputational risks that can undercut global efforts to scale up aid in support of poverty reduction. For these reasons, public sector governance and its monitoring have risen to the top of the development agenda.

Over the past decade, our understanding of how better to address the challenge of improving public sector governance has evolved rapidly. We have learned that technocratic, supply-side initiatives to strengthen public management and rule-boundedness increasingly need to be complemented with demand-side approaches to strengthen transparency, participation, and accountability. Many of these new approaches have been pioneered in country programs supported by the World Bank. The new World Bank Group Strategy, *Strengthening Bank Group Engagement on Governance and Anticorruption,* is a determined effort to systematize and scale up what we have learned. The strategy is broad: it focuses on both governance and anticorruption, and proposes initiatives to address them at global, country, and project levels. This volume focuses on a subset of the agenda, namely country-level initiatives to improve governance and thereby fight corruption.

The volume has its antecedent in the 2006 Global Monitoring Report, *Strengthening Mutual Accountability.* Part II of the GMR focused on "Governance as Part of Global Monitoring." This volume offers further detail of the GMR's governance analysis, extending the ideas and laying out some operational implications.

The ideas in this volume are those of the author, not formal World Bank policy (though they are, of course, consistent with the new Bank strategy). They have been discussed extensively across the World Bank; numerous Bank governance practitioners and analysts have provided inputs. I thus commend the volume to readers both as an analytical piece in its own right, and as providing a good sense of the evolving trajectory of World Bank work on governance.

Sanjay Pradhan,
Director, Public Sector Governance Group, and
Chair of the Bank-Wide Public Sector Governance Board
The World Bank

Executive Summary

Developing country governance and its monitoring have risen to the top of the development agenda. The high profile of governance is a response to compelling evidence that links the quality of a governance system with its development performance. It is also a consequence of the commitment by the world's nations to the principle of mutual accountability: donors commit to scale up resource flows to developing countries; recipient countries commit to ensuring that aid is used effectively toward reaching the Millennium Development Goals (MDGs), and corruption is contained.

As a contribution to addressing this operational challenge, Part II of the 2006 *Global Monitoring Report* (GMR) focused on "governance as part of global monitoring." This publication reproduces—in a self-standing and expanded form—that part of the GMR that focused on developing country governance. The self-standing piece aims to make the analysis available in a form that is more naturally accessible to development practitioners focused on governance—and to amplify it with material that is better suited to a specialist audience than to the GMR readership.

The first section of this executive summary presents a framework for monitoring, identifies indicators that are useful for monitoring the different parts of the framework, and highlights some of the opportunities—and perils—that confront the governance monitoring exercise. Together, the framework, the indicators, and the overview of governance monitoring set the stage for more disaggregated analysis. Section II focuses on monitoring and reform of the key cross-cutting control systems of public bureaucracies—public finance and administrative management. Section III examines some options for monitoring and reform of checks-and-balances institutions. Section IV focuses on governance reform from the front-line perspective of how to strengthen service provision and the investment climate. The final section highlights some implications of the diversity of country governance patterns and governance reform options that emerge in the study.

I: Monitoring Developing Country Governance

A monitoring framework

Public sector governance can be defined as the way the state acquires and exercises its authority to provide and manage public goods and services, including regulatory services. A governance system has both a supply side (the capabilities and organizational arrangements embodied in its players) and a demand side (the accountability arrangements that link the players to one another). To monitor governance—and to improve it—a framework is needed to cut through the complexity. Figure 1 outlines one possible framework, which identifies the key actors in a national governance system and the key accountability relationships among them:

- Political leaders are the prime drivers, setting the objectives for the rest of the governance system. Often they work for the general interest; other times they cater to special interests and core supporters. Sometimes these powerful interests may capture the state. Even a democratic electoral process does not guarantee that politicians will focus on the general interest.

FIGURE 1   National Governance Systems—Actors and Accountabilities

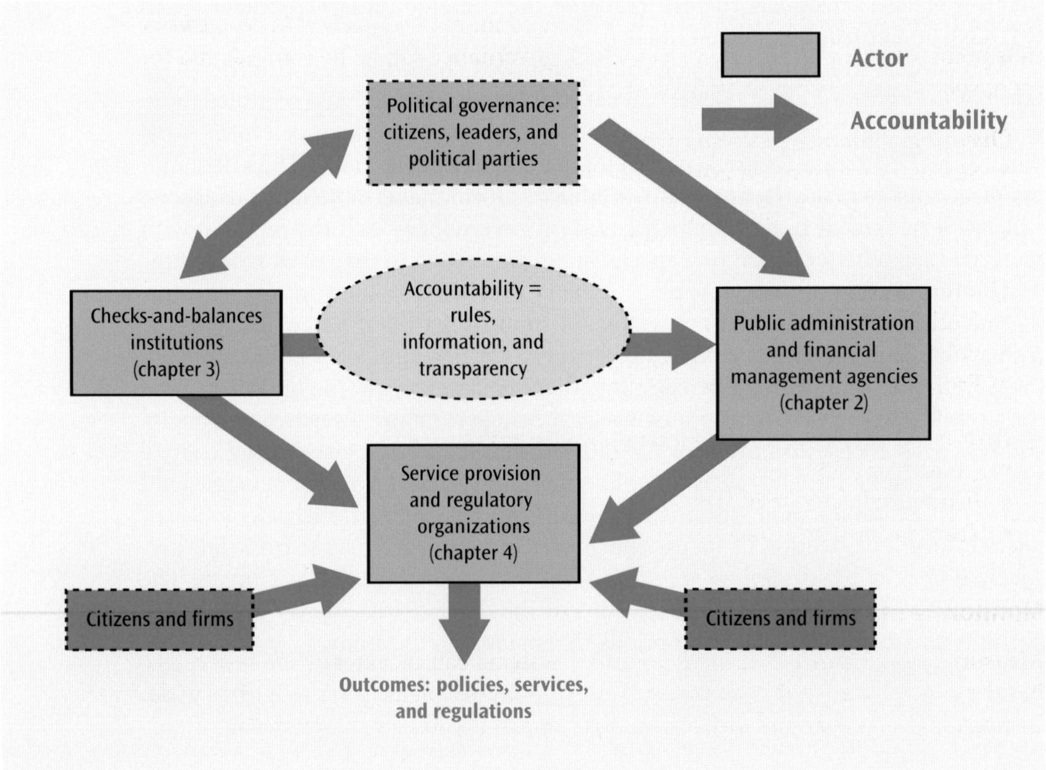

Source: Author.

- Checks-and-balances institutions are important for the sustainability of effective governance. They include parliaments, independent oversight agencies (audit institutions, ombudsmen, and anticorruption commissions), the judicial system, a free press, and accountable local governments.
- The public bureaucracy is the implementing arm of government. It includes both cross-cutting public administration and financial management control agencies (such as the ministry of finance) and agencies that directly deliver social and regulatory services to citizens and firms (for example, education or licensing).
- Citizens and firms are central to effective accountability. Citizens select political leaders. As users of services, citizens and firms can also hold providers accountable for the efficiency and effectiveness of service provision.

Within such a system, effective accountability requires clear rules and expectations, transparent information to monitor performance, and incentives and enforcement mechanisms that reward success and address failure. Transparency is not sufficient on its own for good governance, but it is a powerful feature for improvement, with broad applicability across an array of public actions. Corruption is one outcome of a governance system. It can reflect the failure of any number of accountability relationships, such as political failure leading to state capture, bureaucratic failure, or a failure of checks and balances.

While it may be difficult to get more than a subjective measure of political governance, the capability of the bureaucracy, the strength of checks and balances, and some aspects of service delivery can be measured more objectively. The framework thus points to three different ways in which governance can be monitored, and for each, specific foci for measurement are suggested:

- *Overall governance performance:*
  - Summary measures of governance system quality
  - Control of corruption
  - Quality of economic and sectoral policies

- *Quality of bureaucracy:*
  - Public financial management and procurement systems
  - Public administrative systems
  - Front-line service provision and regulatory agencies

- *Performance of checks-and-balances institutions:*
  - Constraints on the executive
  - Justice and the rule of law
  - Transparency and voice

Monitoring indicators

Measuring governance is difficult. Formal systems can be categorized and rated, but the gap between formal arrangements and realities on the ground is often wide. Institutional processes are difficult to observe and measure systematically.

One approach is to use broad measures to monitor aggregate governance. The study highlights several useful aggregate indicators, including the so-called Kaufmann-Kraay (KK) indicators compiled by the World Bank Institute on the basis of a large number of (mostly external) assessments, Transparency International (TI) indicators, and the Country Policy and Institutional Assessments (CPIAs) compiled by the World Bank (the 2005 ratings have been released for International Development Association [IDA] countries).

These broad governance indicators have many uses. They can be powerful forces for raising awareness, and they can also focus attention on broad areas in which individual countries can strengthen their national systems. However, these broad indicators, as with all governance indicators, are also subject to quite wide measurement errors.

By ranking countries on the basis of the KK corruption indicators, for example, only 87 out of 203 can be confidently assigned to top, middle, and bottom thirds. The standard measurement error in the CPIA is of a similar relative magnitude. Assessments can therefore broadly distinguish high-, middle-, and low-rated countries, but some are likely to be misclassified when ratings are broken down on a much finer scale. Governance indicators also may not be able to pick up with precision the modest, short-run changes in governance, although they will do better at signaling longer-run trends. In sum, broad governance indicators are useful, but have limitations, including their margins of error; as a basis for cross-country comparison, they need to be applied with caution.

A second approach is to use narrow measures of the quality of specific governance subsystems. While these, too, can have nontrivial measurement error, the narrow focus of specific indicators makes them "actionable" in the sense that they can help to identify governance weaknesses and to monitor improvements. Specific governance indicators are being used in diverse ways:

- The Public Expenditure and Financial Accountability (PEFA) program uses 28 indicators to track public financial management.
- The Doing Business (DB) and Investment Climate Surveys (ICS) are creating monitoring baselines for regulatory performance, including a baseline for corruption.
- The Global Integrity Index (GII) assesses checks-and-balances arrangements to prevent the abuse of power, promote public integrity, and assure citizens access to their government in over 50 countries.
- Detailed indicators have been developed for monitoring procurement, the quality of statistical systems, and administrative reform.
- User scorecards and similar surveys provide an entry point into governance from the perspective of service delivery.

So far, however, only the indicators related to private sector development and to public financial management are being used systematically in operational governance work.

Between them, the broad and specific approaches to governance monitoring yield 14 governance measures that offer comprehensive country coverage, and cover each of the diverse facets of national governance systems. These measures can provide a useful baseline for ongoing governance monitoring to move forward. The greatest value added for governance monitoring will come from the improvement of specific indicators.

II: Monitoring and Improving Bureaucratic Capability

An effective bureaucracy is important for development. The bureaucracy formulates detailed policies that translate the goals of society and of its political leaders into programs of action, manages the implementation of these policies, and reports on progress. Bureaucratic reform thus addresses both cross-cutting, upstream systems and downstream front-line service provision and regulatory agencies. This section focuses on options for monitoring and improving the upstream systems. Section IV focuses downstream.

Helping to build bureaucratic capability has long been a focus of development assistance. Before 2000, the profile of work remained low, with a gradual accumulation of lessons and advice on good practice. But its profile has risen dramatically, as it has become apparent that better public policy making, financial management, and administration in developing countries would help resolve a seeming contradiction at the heart of the new aid architecture. On the one hand, the willingness of donors to forgive debt and to scale up aid is based on commitments by recipients to focus on poverty reduction in general and the MDGs in particular. On the other hand, the new architecture aims also to build on a hard-learned lesson of development experience—namely that externally imposed "conditionality" generally fails to achieve its intended results. The national budget—plus the public bureaucracy that prepares and implements the budget, and is accountable to its citizens—are the key vehicles for assuring real country ownership and leadership.

Monitoring and improving public financial management

The figure 2 framework for assessing the quality of public finance systems, developed by the Public Expenditure and financial accountability (PEFA) partnership program, depicts four facets of the budget cycle.

- Policy-based budgeting—the formulating process for translating public policies, including policies that emerge from a poverty reduction strategy (PRS) process, into specific budgeted expenditures
- Arrangements for predictability, control, and stewardship in the use of public funds (for example, payroll and procurement systems)
- Systems of accounting and recordkeeping to provide information for proper management and accountability
- External audit and other mechanisms that ensure external scrutiny of the operations of the executive (for example, by parliament)

Comprehensiveness of budget coverage and transparency of fiscal and budget information cut across these four facets. The framework also identifies credibility—that the budget is realistic and implemented as intended—as a key intermediate outcome, a result of the operation of the whole cycle.

Assessments of the quality of budget and financial management systems conducted in both 2001 and 2004 for 22 heavily indebted poor countries (HIPC) showed that, while progress is uneven, countries that are determined to improve their public financial management systems can do so quite rapidly. Six countries, including Ghana, Mali, Senegal, and Tanzania, achieved substantial improvements between 2001 and 2004 (figure 3). With political commitment and support, many countries should be able to achieve reasonably strong public financial management (PFM) within a 5- to 10-year period.

FIGURE 2 Public Financial Management—A Performance Monitoring Framework

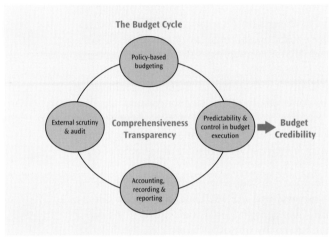

Source: PEFA Secretariat 2005, 4.

A first lesson for strengthening public financial management systems is that in most countries, the approach should be incremental. Countries with committed developmental leadership, plus a preexisting baseline of capacity, appear able to adopt and rapidly implement a comprehensive program of budget reform, to the point that country systems can provide a robust platform for ensuring effectiveness in the use of resources. But where capacity is weaker, there is a need to set realistic goals for what is achievable and implement them in a realistic sequence. The new "platform approach," piloted in Cambodia, involves a cumulative sequence of budget reforms that focuses each round on achieving specific budget functionalities, then building on these functionalities in the subsequent round. The Cambodian platform sequence focuses first on the basics: budget credibility, then predictability and control in budget execution. Only after these first two platforms are locked in will they move on to medium-term budget planning, and only once that is in place will they foster public management reforms to support a results culture throughout the public bureaucracy.

A second emerging lesson for budget management is to complement the technocratic supply-side reforms with greater transparency—and emphasize the potential of public information to improve the developmental discourse among citizens, their governments, and development partners.

Monitoring and improving administrative capability

Some consensus has been generated on the characteristics of an effective public administration. The standard prescription typically includes the following:

■ Well-functioning mechanisms for policy coordination that ensure policy consistency across departmental boundaries and facilitate clear decisions on policy and

FIGURE 3   Net Change in HIPC Indicator Tracking Scores, 2001–04

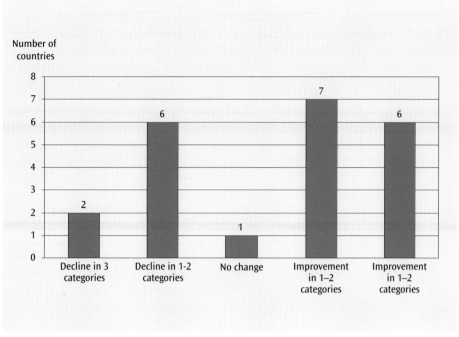

Source: IDA and IMF 2005, appendix 1.

spending priorities. To be effective, these coordinating mechanisms need to be at the apex of government, supported by top political leadership.

■ Well-designed administrative structures for individual line ministries and semi-autonomous executive agencies, with little duplication of responsibility, and with clear lines of authority—plus streamlined business processes and a focus on results.

■ Human resource management underpinned by the principle of meritocracy—including for recruitment, promotion, and major disciplinary actions. This includes insulation from undue political or personal interests, as well as practices that reward good performance (for example, through career advancement and financial rewards) and penalize poor performance.

■ Pay and benefits adequate to attract and retain competent staff, including at senior and technical levels.

■ Establishment and wage bill control over aggregate wage bill sufficiently robust to ensure that the public sector wage bill is sustainable under overall fiscal constraints.

The track record of efforts to close the gaps between the desired and actual quality of public administration is (to put it gently) uneven in both developed and developing countries. A landmark review of public administrative reform in 10 OECD countries—including such noted public management reformers as Australia, New Zealand, Sweden, the United States, and the United Kingdom—concluded:[1]

Reform-watching in public management can be a sobering pastime. The gaps between rhetoric and actions...are frequently so wide as to provoke skepticism. The pace of underlying, embedded achievement tends to be much slower than the helter-skelter cascade of new announcements and initiatives. Incremental analysis and partisan mutual adjustment seem to have been very frequent features of public management reform, even if more-than-incremental changes were frequently hoped for.

In developing countries, public administrative systems are weaker than their budget management counterparts. Monitoring data suggest that, though change generally comes slowly, committed countries can achieve quite rapid improvement in their systems of public administration: The measured improvements between 2001 and 2004 for Armenia, Azerbaijan, Cameroon, Georgia, and Vietnam exceeded any plausible margin of error.

For the reform of public administration, the central lessons parallel that for financial management: achieve a good fit, aligning the administrative reform agenda in a realistic way to a country's political realities on the ground. Proceed with rapid, comprehensive administrative reform only in those rare cases where there is a strong enough baseline of capacity for sustained administrative reform and political leadership with the commitment, mandate, and time horizon needed to see the effort through. (Latvia and Tanzania provide successful examples of quite comprehensive reform). Without such capacity and leadership, the approaches have to be more modest. The example of Albania illustrates how, even in these more difficult settings, carefully designed incremental reforms can achieve quite significant results.

III: Monitoring and Improving National Checks-and-Balances Institutions

Strong checks-and-balances institutions are key to a well-functioning national governance system. Developmental leadership or a dynamic political movement can sometimes substitute for weak checks and balances, at least for a period. But over the longer run, well-functioning checks-and-balances institutions are key to *sustainability*. They help keep the executive arm of government focused on the public purpose. They are vital for fighting corruption, for ensuring that state actors at all levels use public resources efficiently and effectively, and for helping to ensure that citizens perceive state institutions to be legitimate.

Figure 4 disaggregates checks and balances into a constellation, arranged in terms of their "distance" from the executive authority they oversee. The relationship of these institutions with one another is only loosely hierarchical. Depending on a country's constitution, the judiciary may or may not be a constraint on legislative authority. Citizens may ultimately elect governments, but on a day-to-day basis their role is more participatory than hierarchical.

The study examines options for monitoring and reform of checks-and-balances institutions for three broad groups:

- An "inner constellation" of direct oversight—subnational governments, autonomous oversight agencies, and the legislature
- A "middle constellation" of impartial dispute resolution—in particular the justice system
- An "outer constellation" of civic voice—the rules (for example on freedom of information) and actors (such as the media) that ensure the open operation of civil society, and the transparent flow of information and data that enable citizens to play an informed role in public discourse. (Though not an explicit focus in this GMR, the discipline provided by competitive markets is an important buttress of this outer constellation.)

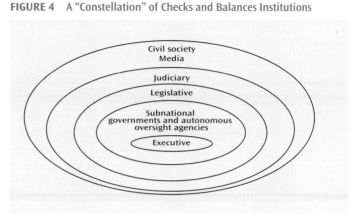

FIGURE 4 A "Constellation" of Checks and Balances Institutions

Source: Author.

Three key themes emerge from the analysis of approaches to monitoring the quality of the relevant checks-and-balances institutions and highlighting how some can be strengthened:

- First, measurement of checks-and-balances institutions confronts a similar tension between broad and specific indicators, as does measurement in other governance areas. Useful broad measures exist for each of the three checks-and-balances constellations: the University of Maryland Polity IV database measure of "Executive Constraints" for direct oversight; and the Kaufmann-Kraay Rule of Law and Voice and Accountability measures for the outer two constellations. As elsewhere, "actionable" indicators, capable of drilling down to identify strengths and weaknesses at increasing levels of disaggregation, seem especially useful. The Global Integrity Index, prepared by the independent nongovernmental organization (NGO), Global Integrity, is a promising initiative to develop actionable checks-and-balances indicators.
- Second, knowledge of how to strengthen formal checks-and-balances institutions remains rudimentary. One emerging lesson is that formal arrangements are embedded within a larger political economy. Dysfunctional institutions are not generally amenable to technocratic quick fixes.
- Third, transparency appears to hold special promise as a relatively low-cost and low-key way of initiating a cumulative process of improvement in public debate, public advocacy, and government accountability to civil society. Its role in national governance systems is pervasive—from the political apex of the system,

through the publication of judicial decisions, to a free press, and all the way to the service provision front line. Transparency has a supply side and a demand side. On the supply side, quality information built on a platform of robust statistical capacity is key, as is assuring that citizens enjoy a right to information. On the demand side, an active civil society is key to translating transparent information into action.

IV: Governance Reform at the Front Line— Service Provision and the Investment Climate

Top-down reforms of bureaucracies and checks-and-balances institutions generally take a long time before they help improve the front-line performance of governments. Low-income countries seeking to turn around their performance thus confront a dilemma. Maintaining the momentum of a turnaround may depend on achieving major gains in service provision in the short to medium term. But reforming their formal top-down state accountability system to the point that it can provide the requisite combination of accountability and responsiveness is a task that will bear fruit only over the long run.

In the face of this dilemma, it is natural to complement top-down reforms with approaches that work more directly at the interface between governments on the one hand, and citizens and firms on the other, including: *the provision of services* to citizens and firms, such as education, health care, utilities, transport infrastructure, and the like; *credible commitment* to private investors as to the stability of the rules of the game; and *credible regulation* of markets as well as criminal activity and other antisocial behavior.

Top-down and front-line approaches often are perceived to be at odds with each other. A contrasting perspective is that their relationship can be mutually reinforcing. Front-line approaches have the potential to help address a weakness of top-down reforms: aside from the long lags before they deliver results, top-down initiatives can be undercut insofar as they are not underpinned by a change in the incentives of political and bureaucratic leaders. They are "upstream," without well-defined front-line actors (firms, citizens, civil society organizations, service users, and so forth) to push for results. Especially in weaker governance settings, where expectations and top-down pressures for improved performance may be limited, engaging at the front line has the potential to alter this equation—achieving development results quite quickly, while also potentially helping to accelerate the pressure and momentum for deeper top-down reforms.

Two sets of challenges are key to achieving development effectiveness via the front line—getting the priorities right, and getting the accountabilities right. Getting the priorities right is key, because the front-line agenda of governments is a broad one—too broad to be addressed comprehensively in countries with limited resources and capacities. Getting the accountabilities right is key to assuring that front-line agencies use the resources allocated to them well.

Getting the priorities right

Approaches to prioritizing are evolving in similar ways in work on public expenditure management and the investment climate. In both areas, the standard approach has been a cross-cutting one. But this approach does not reckon either with capacity limitations, or with political obstacles that limit the domain of feasible reforms. Consequently, the focus of reform recently has shifted toward more targeted approaches that aim to identify and act on specific high-return opportunities.

For public spending, while the returns are high from cross-cutting efforts to strengthen budget systems so governments can prioritize more effectively, especially in low-income and weaker governance settings the need to use resources well is too urgent to be dependent solely on systemic improvements. The case is compelling for complementing efforts at system improvements with more targeted efforts—within individual sectors and across sectors—to identify high-return investment opportunities, plus opportunities for freeing up resources locked into low-return activities. This is an activity for which development partners can provide targeted assistance. The Public Expenditure Reviews facilitated by the World Bank—already an established part of the landscape of development dialogue—offer a ready-made vehicle.

For investment climate reforms, their components are many and varied, including macro stability, property rights, reduced crime, business regulation, tax and trade policy, financial markets, infrastructure, workforce quality, industrial policy, and labor market regulation. Which of these factors is likely to be a binding constraint to private sector-led growth will vary across countries and over time. But whatever the constraint, it is likely to need governance reforms to be addressed effectively:

- Easing constraints linked to low social returns—bad infrastructure and low human capital—needs better bureaucratic capability and better accountability.
- Easing constraints linked to government failures and associated weaknesses in credible commitment—the protection of property rights and control of corruption—needs better checks-and-balances institutions.
- Easing constraints linked to market failures needs proactive, market-enhancing government interventions. To be effective, market-enhancing interventions generally require a capable state—both high levels of bureaucratic capability and skillful use of discretionary authority by implementing agencies.

Comparative country surveying and benchmarking seem a natural way to identify country-specific constraints to growth. But the implications of country-specific data may be more nuanced than they first appear. As table 1 shows, Kenya, Bangladesh, and Tanzania score poorly on measures of the quality of some de jure rules for doing business, with Kenya rating perhaps a little better than the others. But survey evidence of the de facto realities on the ground in the three countries does not correspond to these de jure patterns. Tanzania's de jure rigidities indeed signal a rigid business environment. By contrast, Bangladesh's business environment is lubricated by corruption. Corruption is also rife in Kenya. Unlike in Bangladesh, though, the lubricating impact of Kenya's corruption seems limited.

TABLE 1   Transactions Costs of Doing Business—DB and ICS Results

	Kenya	Bangladesh	Tanzania
De jure rules (DB country rank)			
Starting a business	93	52	113
Dealing with licenses	15	53	150
Registering property	113	151	143
Trading across borders	126	125	102
Corruption (ICS)			
Bribes/Sales (%)	2.9%	2.1%	1.3%
Gifts in meetings with tax officials (% firms)	37.0%	86.0%	22.4%
Gift value (% government contract)	6.5%	4.0%	2.9%
De facto burden (ICS)			
Senior management time dealing with regulations (%)	11.7%	3.7%	14.4%
Time spent with tax officials (days)	4	2	12
Average time to clear exports through customs (days)	4	8	10
Average time to claim imports from customs (days)	8	10	15

Sources: www.doingbusiness.org; www.enterprisesurveys.org.

Once binding constraints on growth and priority areas for public spending are identified, a natural followup is to focus implementation on these areas. One approach is to focus effort on a single sector (chapter 4 discusses roads and schools). Focusing public management reforms sectorally has the potential to achieve multiple goals simultaneously:

- achieving some quick wins in a high-priority area
- in weaker governance settings, providing a mechanism for using the limited country capacity for policy formulation and implementation in a focused way
- providing a clear focal point for results-based monitoring and evaluation, thereby helping assure mutual accountability on the part of donors and the recipient government and ministry

Focusing public management reforms on a single sector runs the risk of making systemic reform more difficult later on. But this presumes that broader systemic reforms are directly feasible; in most early turnaround situations this is unlikely to be the case. The challenge is to achieve gains in an imperfect world, where the best can be the enemy of the good.

For the investment climate, the most widespread example of responding to capacity limitations (and political constraints) by narrowing the focus of reform comprises the targeted promotion of exports. Export processing zones (EPZs) are one example. By the end of 2002, some 3,000 EPZs had been created in 116 countries, providing jobs for some 43 million workers, most of them women. Paralleling the dilemma for sector-specific public management reforms, targeted approaches to promote exports face the challenge of assuring that they link to the broader economy and do not end up as dead-end islands of effectiveness amid a nonreforming sea of continuing private sector backwardness. Many countries establish special programs designed to foster spillovers from foreign direct investment, with the "linkage" programs of Singapore and Ireland being notably successful.

Getting the accountabilities right

This can be challenging, and the challenges are different in strong and weak governance settings. In OECD countries, the principal challenge is to reshape the formal, top-down accountability straitjacket in ways that enable providers to be more responsive to users. By contrast, the legacy in many low-income settings is not so much excess control as it is excess informality—weak controls, arbitrary discretion at all levels of the bureaucracy, and corruption.

The effort to assert top-down accountability without straitjacketing front-line agencies with excessively rigid rules has been a key theme of efforts at public management reform in many OECD countries—from New Zealand's pioneering experiments, to the American Reinventing Government initiative, to myriad other experiments under the New Public Management label. It has also been a central preoccupation of efforts to assure efficient private participation and regulation in electricity, water and other infrastructure utilities.

A very different approach is to try to get results at the front line by complementing top-down efforts with more bottom-up approaches to participation and accountability. The approach is relevant everywhere, with special salience in set-

FIGURE 5 Perceptions of Service Delivery Performance in Nine Bangalore Agencies, 1994–2003

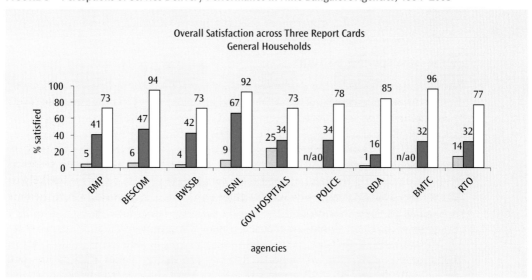

Source: Samuel Paul, Public Affairs Centre, Bangalore, presentation at 6th Global Forum on "Reinventing Governments."
Note: BMP = Bangalore Municipal Corporation; BESCOM = electricity; BWSSB = water supply; BSNL = telecommunications department;
BDA = land development authority; BMTC = metropolitan transport coRPORATION; RTO = motor vehicle licensing

tings where top-down state capabilities and accountabilities are weak. One way of fostering bottom-up accountability is to use citizen engagement in the collection and dissemination of information on service quality and resource use to build demand for better services and more accountability. To illustrate, consider Bangalore, India. Frustrated by years of inaction on public services, which increasingly were unable to keep up with Bangalore's dynamism and population pressure, in 1994 a group of citizens introduced the idea of a user survey-based "report card" on public services. Initially, the impact was modest. Nonetheless, the sponsors persisted, establishing a nongovernmental organization, the Bangalore Public Affairs Center, to institutionalize the effort, building coalitions with other NGOs and repeating the report card survey in 1999 and 2003. Figure 5 highlights the extraordinary turnaround in perceptions of the quality of service delivery.

Another way of fostering bottom-up accountability is to engage citizens more directly in service provision via community-driven development (CDD). As with many donor-funded initiatives, early generation efforts to get resources to communities bypassed the public administration, with the usual pernicious effects of parallel implementation. Learning from these experiences, practitioners of CDD have worked to design and implement programs as part of a broader strategy of governance improvement, combining scaled-up participatory resource transfers to communities and longer-run institutional reform by working closely with line ministries and local governments to help build their capabilities and interactions with community groups. The jury remains out as to the impact of this hybrid approach.

V: Governance Reform—Country Patterns and Reform Options

This final section of the executive summary suggests some ways to make sense of the diversity of country governance patterns and governance reform options.

Some cross-country patterns

Individual countries show a strikingly uneven mix of strengths and weaknesses across different governance subsystems and governance-related outcomes. For the two outcomes (corruption and policy quality), as table 2 shows, country performance is broadly similar for 34 of the 66 IDA-eligible countries. But, even making substantial allowance for the margins of error in measurement, in 17 countries the quality of policy and institutions is better than performance on corruption, and 15 countries show the opposite pattern. Bangladesh currently is perhaps the best-known example of a country with relatively weak perceived control of corruption, but strong performance on policies and on poverty reduction—though, as table 2 suggests, many other countries evince a similar pattern.

Paralleling these differences in performance are differences in the quality of governance subsystems. Table 3 identifies 28 countries that rate well in either the quality of their bureaucracies or their checks-and-balances institutions. While 10 countries rate well in both areas, performance across the remaining countries is

TABLE 2   Intermediate Outcomes—Corruption Versus Policy

	CPIA 2004 policy quintiles (cluster a-c average)				
	Bottom quintile	4th quintile	3rd quintile	2nd quintile	Top quintile
Control of corruption and policy performance are broadly similar	Angola, Central African Republic, Comoros, Congo, Dem. Rep. of, Côte d'Ivoire, Lao PDR, Nigeria, Solomon Islands, Sudan	Burundi, Cambodia, Congo, Rep. of, Djibouti, Papua New Guinea, Sierra Leone, Zambia	Cameroon, Ethiopia, Kenya, Malawi, Moldova, Nepal, Rwanda, Mozambique, Yemen, Rep. of, Niger	Benin, Bosnia and Herzegovina, Mali, Serbia and Montenegro, Sri Lanka	Burkina Faso, Nicaragua, Senegal
Better policies, weaker control of corruption		Chad, Haiti, Uzbekistan	Tajikistan	Bangladesh, Georgia, Kyrgyz Republic, Indonesia, Vietnam	Albania, Armenia, Azerbaijan, Bolivia, Honduras, Pakistan, Tanzania, Uganda
Better corruption control, less good policies	Eritrea, Guinea-Bissau, São Tomé and Principe, Togo, Zimbabwe	Gambia, The, Guinea, Mauritania	Mongolia, Lesotho	Bhutan, Ghana, Guyana, India, Madagascar	

Sources: World Bank 2004 CPIA Database; Kaufmann, Kraay, Zoido-Lobaton 2005.
a. Country percentile rank for the CPIA Policy Outcome and the Kaufmann, Kraay, and Zoido-Lobaton (KKZ) Control of Corruption indicator are less than 20 percentile points apart.
b. Country percentile rank for Policy Outcome is better than Control of Corruption by percentile rank of at least 20 points.
c. Country percentile rank for Control of Corruption is better than Policy Outcome by percentile rank of at least 20 points.

uneven. Ten countries (Rwanda and Vietnam, for example) have relatively capable public bureaucracies, but less strong checks-and-balances institutions. And the pattern is reversed in the other eight countries (Albania and Lesotho, for instance), where relatively stronger indicators for checks and balances are not matched by correspondingly capable public bureaucracies.

Sequencing governance reforms

Why might patterns such as those in tables 2 and 3 be observed? Figure 6 illustrates three possible trajectories for governance turnarounds. In the first trajectory (Indonesia in the 1970s and Uganda in the 1980s are examples), a political leader takes power who focuses on liberalizing the economy and strengthening the performance of the public sector—with checks and balances a lower priority. Poverty reduction gains can be rapid in this scenario, but if country reformers and development partners wait too long to put the challenge of strengthening checks and bal-

TABLE 3   State Capacity and State Accountability, 2004

Bureaucratic capability	Quality of checks-and-balances institutions	
	Medium or Low	Higher
Higher	10 countries (Azerbaijan, Bhutan, Burkina Faso, Ethiopia, Indonesia, Pakistan, Rwanda, Tanzania, Uganda, Vietnam)	10 countries (Armenia, Benin, Bolivia, Ghana, Honduras, India, Mali, Senegal, Serbia and Montenegro, Sri Lanka)
Medium or Low	38 countries	8 countries (Albania, Guyana, Lesotho, Moldova, Mongolia, Nicaragua, Niger, Papua New Guinea)

Source: Collated by authors.
Notes: States with higher bureaucratic capability are those with CPIA-budget scores of 4 and above, or both CPIA-admin and CPIA-budget scores of 3.5 and above. States with higher quality of checks-and-balances institutions are those which score "high" on at least two of checks-and-balances measures in Tables 3.1, 3.3 and 3.6.

ances onto the agenda, the consequence (as in Indonesia during the latter Suharto years) can be rising corruption, financial crisis, a difficult process of political succession, and a reversal of earlier gains.

In the second trajectory, a country moves to political pluralism (for example, Albania in the early 1990s and Nigeria more recently). Only sometimes does this new political openness translate into stronger bureaucratic capability. In the third trajectory, following state collapse, international intervention or support helps to provide an umbrella of security under which both the bureaucracy and checks-and-balances institutions are reestablished (Mozambique offers an example of a country that appears to have followed a balanced trajectory).

These varying trajectories pose some dilemmas for the design and sequencing of governance reform:

- Change that focuses first on improvements in bureaucratic quality has the potential for rapid gains in public sector performance. But without a subsequent effort to strengthen checks-and-balances institutions, it risks subsequent reversal—perhaps by a reversion to corrupt behavior by the political leadership, perhaps by a loss of legitimacy with citizens.
- Change that begins with a political opening can generate a surge of confidence and improve the climate for private investment. But unless the gains are consolidated, the country risks becoming trapped in a cycle of what Thomas Carothers (Carothers 2002) has called "feckless pluralism," with short-lived governments repeatedly voted out of power, never having sufficient support and longevity to build the base of bureaucratic capability on which effectiveness and legitimacy will eventually depend.

FIGURE 6 Governance Turnarounds—Three Trajectories

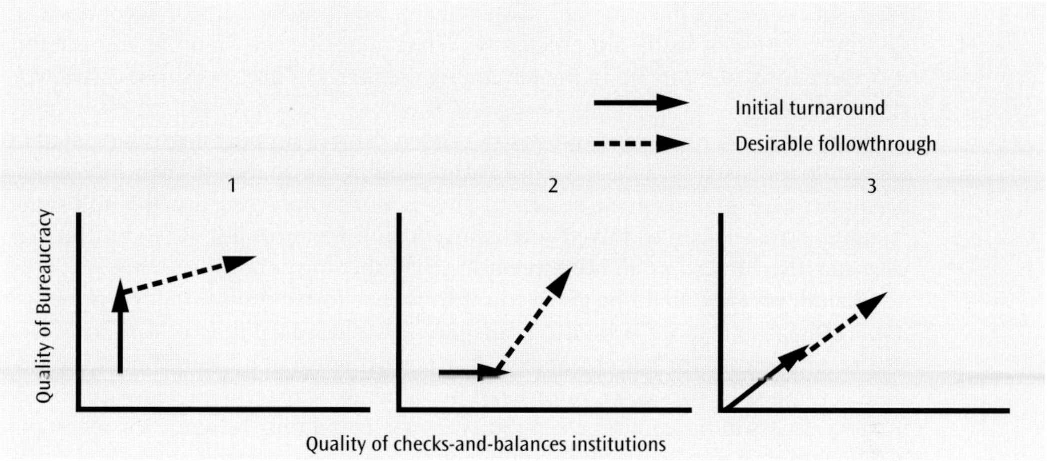

Quality of checks-and-balances institutions

Source: Author.

Development partners need to take the different governance trajectories into account and to engage, on a long-term basis in strengthening lagging elements of the governance system. It took many years for durable governance institutions to emerge in today's industrial countries.

What is the role of front-line-focused approaches in the sequencing of governance reform? As noted, they can be viewed as part of a mutually reinforcing spiral of top-down and bottom-up change. Engaging from the bottom up has the potential to alter the incentives of upstream political and bureaucratic leaders in ways that spur top-down improvements:

■ Sector-specific approaches to improve service provision can have positive demonstration effects, with the potential to spur change more broadly.
■ Export-focused reforms of the investment climate can help crowd in new private firms with the incentive and clout to push for continuing improvements.
■ Approaches that enhance transparency and participation empower users of services (citizens, firms, and communities) to press for better public performance.

Viewed as a whole, the strategy of governance reform suggested by this study can be described as one of "orchestrated imbalance." Imbalance builds momentum by embracing entry points for reform that have development impact in the short term, and also ratchet up tension in the governance system. Orchestration helps assure that binding supply-side public management constraints are addressed before they short-circuit the entire process of change. Throughout, monitoring is crucial to assure progress on the immediate governance agenda, and to uncover the next round of binding constraints.

What all these means for scaling up aid

Governance reform is a work in progress. Interpreting "good enough governance" expansively, governance indicators suggest that only a minority of low-income aid recipients currently have budget management, administrative, and accountability systems capable of using aid efficiently. What might be the "mutual accountability" basis for scalingup aid in the remaining countries? Three possibilities are worthy of note:

First, even where current systems fall short, budget support might be scaled up for countries based on a clearly improving trend in the quality of their budget and administrative management systems. This is not simply because the additional resource transfers can be poverty reducing: A shift from project aid to budget support can also be seen as an investment in strengthening country systems.[2]

Second, priority could be given to reforms that foster transparency—in budget management and more broadly. Transparency relies on public information as a source of pressure for better public sector performance in a less technocratic way than is implied by top-down reforms of bureaucratic capability. Even with continuing weakness in bureaucratic capability, a case could thus be made for scaling up aid (including some component of budget support) to countries that clearly commit themselves to facilitating transparency in how public resources—and state power more broadly—are used.

The third possibility for countries is to target scaled-up aid more directly toward poverty-reducing services, which can be done in several ways. A key distinction here is between countries where bureaucratic capability may be on the upturn but is only at an early stage of improvement, and those where there is little sign of political commitment to improve governance and capacity. In the former group, sectorwide approaches that focus on improving governance and service provision in part of the overall system are attractive. In the latter group, the focus might be on infrastructure and other service delivery investment projects, complete with project implementation units and related mechanisms that operate apart from country systems. There are some well-founded objections to these approaches. But where there is little political commitment to improve country systems and little sign that governments would have targeted pro-poor spending, these objections have less relevance.

Notes

1. Pollitt and Bouckaert 2000, 184, 188–89.
2. See Gelb and Eifert (2005) for this argument.

1

Monitoring
Developing Country
Governance

Introduction

Developing country governance and its monitoring have risen to the top of the development agenda. This high profile is a response to compelling evidence that links the quality of a governance system with its development performance. It is also a consequence of the commitment by the world's nations to the principle of mutual accountability: donors commit to scaling up resource flows to developing countries; recipient countries commit to ensuring that aid is used effectively toward reaching the MDGs; and corruption is contained. The challenge of moving beyond general affirmations of the importance of governance to pragmatic ways forward is, however, proving to be formidable.

As a contribution to addressing this operational challenge, Part II of the 2006 GMR focused on "governance as part of global monitoring." This publication reproduces—in a self-standing and expanded form—that part of the GMR analysis that focused on developing country governance. A first purpose of this self-standing piece is to make the analysis available in a form that is more naturally accessible to development practitioners focused on governance. A second purpose is to amplify the analysis with material that is better suited to a specialist audience than to the GMR readership.

Strong empirical evidence links governance to growth. The relationships are robust both over time—as, for example, in the thousand-year evolution of governance systems that underpin today's developed countries—and across countries, as evident in many multicountry econometric studies (see box 1.1).

■ Careful econometric work shows that the benefits of public health spending on child and infant mortality rates are significantly greater in countries with better governance and that, as countries improve their governance, public spending on

BOX 1.1   Governance and Growth—the Big Picture

Empirical research over the past decade has compellingly demonstrated the impact of good governance on growth, both for today's developing countries and over the past millennium for countries that are now regarded as developed.

De Long and Shleifer (1993) found that absolutist government is associated with slow growth of cities in the 800 years leading up to the Industrial Revolution. They classified by type of regime each of nine regions in Western Europe for each of five periods from 1050 to 1800. "Absolutist states are characterized by the subjection of the legal framework to the prince's will." Good examples of these are France under Louis XIV and Spain under Philip II. Nonabsolutist regimes in their sample have "more restrictive governments" that generally "give a voice or a constitutional veto to merchants or assemblies of landed magnates..." (674). Examples include constitutional monarchies such as Britain in the aftermath of the Glorious Revolution, merchant ruled city-states such as the Venetian and Florentine republics, and feudal governments in which kings or emperors were not always able to impose their authority on dukes or city-states. In the absence of data on incomes, De Long and Shleifer used city size as an indicator of commercial prosperity. They found that on average, for each century of absolutist rule in a region, the number of people living in large cities (those with a population of 30,000 or more) in the region is 180,000 less than it would have been with a nonabsolutist government. The clearest example in their study is that of the Low Countries in the 16th and 17th centuries, where the Habsburgs succeeded in establishing long-term absolutist rule only in the south (which became Belgium). An explosion of economic growth in the north (which became the Netherlands) followed the Dutch revolt, along with a large migration from Antwerp to Amsterdam over the period 1570–1620 (De Long and Shleifer, 1993, 696–97).

For the contemporary era, evidence from large cross-country samples, based on recent data and including numerous less-developed nations, was provided by Barro (1991), Mauro (1995), and Knack and Keefer (1995). Barro's (1991) classic empirical study on the determinants of growth tested indicators of political instability, which he interpreted as "adverse influences on property rights." He found that frequencies of revolutions, coups, and political assassinations were significantly and negatively related to growth rates and to private investment's share of GDP over the 1960–85 period, controlling for initial income and other factors. Mauro (1995) and Knack and Keefer (1995) replaced the political violence frequencies with broader, subjective assessments of political risk to overseas investors, provided by commercial firms. These measures of corruption, bureaucratic quality, rule of law, expropriation risk, and so forth, were found to be strongly associated with lower investment and growth rates, and had greater explanatory power than the political violence frequencies.[3]

These statistical findings conceivably are attributable at least in part to reverse causation from economic performance to good governance. Chong and Calderon (2000) find significant causality from good governance to growth, and vice versa. Similarly, Alesina, et al. (1996) found that political instability and economic performance are jointly determined: coups lead to worse economic performance, but slow growth in turn increases the likelihood of coups. A strong test of causality is to measure longer-run growth in incomes during periods entirely subsequent to when the quality-of-governance assessments were made. The strong relationship between governance and growth remains. Moreover, these results are not very sensitive to whether the developed countries are included in the sample. The scatterplot in the box figure below

BOX 1.1   Governance and Growth—the Big Picture (continued)

depicts the partial relationship (controlling for initial income and schooling levels) between the quality of governance in 1982 and income growth from 1982 to 2002. The sample omits 22 developed (donor) nations. The relationship remains statistically significant, although somewhat weakened, when nations in the East Asia and Pacific region are also deleted.[4]

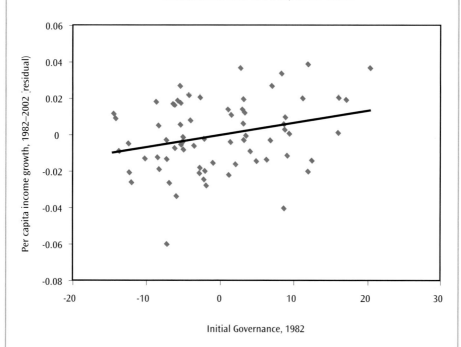

Governance and Growth, 1982–2002

Source: Steve Knack, unpublished note 2005.

primary education becomes more effective in increasing primary education attainment.[5]

■ The scale of corruption has posed extraordinary costs on some countries. A conservative estimate is that the former president of Zaire looted the treasury of some US$5 billion—an amount equal to the country's entire external debt at the time he was ousted in 1997. The funds allegedly embezzled by former presidents of Indonesia and the Philippines are estimated to be two and seven times higher, respectively.[6]

■ Micro-level studies reveal the ubiquitous daily impact of corruption, and the benefits of scaling it back. In health care: During the first nine months of a 1996–7 crackdown on corruption in Buenos Aires, Argentina, the prices paid for basic inputs at public hospitals fell by 15 percent. In customs: The use of private international firms to conduct preshipment inspection of imports are associated with increases in the growth rate of import duties of six to eight points annually.[7]

Are there mechanisms in place to ensure that public resources reach their intended purpose with little leakage or diversion? Is the investment climate supportive of growth and reductions in income poverty? Can countries develop plans and do they have the institutional capacity to execute them? Is there adequate information and transparency in government to foster an active civil society to build greater accountability in government? Are the incentives and accountabilities of service providers adequate to ensure low absenteeism and shirking? Does the rule of law protect the rights of citizens? The answers to these questions depend on the quality of national governance systems.

This study addresses the challenges of governance monitoring and reform in four chapters. The present chapter focuses directly on governance monitoring. It presents a framework for monitoring, identifies indicators that are useful for monitoring the different parts of the framework, and highlights some of the opportunities—and perils—that confront the governance monitoring exercise. Together, these set the stage for more disaggregated analysis in chapters 2 through 4.

Chapter 2 focuses on monitoring and reform of the key cross-cutting control systems of public bureaucracies—public finance and administrative management. Chapter 3 examines some options for monitoring and reform of checks-and balances-institutions. Finally, chapter 4 focuses on governance reform from the frontline perspective of how to strengthen service provision and the investment climate.

A Framework for Monitoring Governance

Because governance is central in development, it is natural that many stakeholders want to monitor it. It is also natural that these stakeholders use governance measures in different ways.

- Citizens and firms in developing countries can use measures of governance to hold governments accountable for their actions—at the micro level for the quality of service provision and the investment climate, at the aggregate level for the responsiveness of government action to the public interest, and at all levels for the probity of using resources.
- Governments in developing countries (and development partners seeking to provide technical support) can use governance measures to improve the design of policy, for example, by providing "actionable" guideposts for operational efforts to improve governance.
- Donors seek assurance that the resources they provide are being well used, not squandered or misappropriated. While some governance weakness is an inevitable part of underdevelopment, providers of resources can reasonably expect evidence that systems are improving. So donors can use governance measures for cross-country comparisons (focusing on "levels" at a point in time), or to monitor the trends within individual countries over time.

Monitoring governance has become a growth industry. A recent publication of the United Nations Development Programme (UNDP 2004), *Governance Indicators: A Users' Guide,* details 33 data sources and lists a further 33 that did not meet UNDP standards for inclusion. This focus on measurement has led to some important advances, but it has also underscored some difficulties.

Governance is more complex than it seems. While the word is often used as a euphemism for corruption, a country's governance system comprises the full array of state institutions and the arrangements that shape the relations between state and society (box 1.2). Measurement can explore the broad consequences of how the governance system functions (with corruption as a major example). It can also focus more narrowly on the quality of the different institutions that make up a country's governance system. Conceptual clarity is needed to draw distinctions between these different types of measures.

A national governance system includes many institutions and actors, including judges, legislators, tax inspectors, teachers, and accountants. Each needs the capacity to perform his or her function effectively. Effective governance also calls for the

---

BOX 1.2   Governance and Corruption Are Not the Same Thing

Governance and corruption often are used synonymously. But they are quite different concepts, and conflating them can be very damaging.

Public sector governance refers to the way that the state acquires and exercises the authority to provide and manage public goods and services, including both public capacities and public accountabilities. Viewed from the perspective of this report, the relevant aspects of governance are those for achieving the MDGs. This narrows the terrain somewhat, but perhaps less than it might seem at first sight, given the relationships among transparency, participation, and accountability on the one hand, and performance in reducing poverty on the other.

Corruption is an outcome. It is a consequence of the failure of any of a number of accountability relationships that characterize a national governance system—from a failure of the citizen-politician relationship (which can lead to state capture), to a failure of bureaucratic and checks–and-balances institutions (which can lead to administrative corruption). Aggregate measures of corruption thus offer a useful overview of the degree to which the national governance system as a whole—rather than any part—is dysfunctional.

Perceptions of corruption can have a profound impact on a country's prospects. At home, they can break (or make) the reputation of political leaders, and affect civic perceptions of the legitimacy and trustworthiness of the state. Globally, these perceptions influence decisions on private capital flows and aid. Estimates of corruption raise awareness and attention, including through media focus on rankings. Even if these estimates have a high margin of error, with movements of a few points in one or another direction too small for any robust implication, they can still be useful. Yet an exclusive focus on this outcome of a governance system has caused some countries to emphasize simple-minded (and largely failed) anticorruption initiatives—to the neglect of the complex challenge of strengthening national governance systems themselves.

Source: Author.

---

players to be accountable, often in complex ways. A school, for example, is potentially accountable to parents, to officials in departments of education (at local and central levels), to courts, and to politicians (again, both national and local).

To monitor governance—and to improve it—a framework is needed to cut through the complexity. Figure 1.1 illustrates one approach. It shows the key actors in a national governance system, and the key accountability relationships that align the incentives of the principals at each level with those of the agents delegated to act for them. As the figure suggests, transparency is an essential cross-cutting aspect of the governance system, contributing to the efficacy of both the actors and the accountability relationships.

For each actor, the relevant capacities comprise the skills adequate for the task at hand, the organizational management systems capable of deploying human and other resources, the transparent provision of the information needed for action, and the leadership to organize the various parts of the system and motivate its participants from the inside. Each accountability relationship rests on the following:

- Rules to delegate authority and indicate constraints and expected results.
- Information flows to enable principals to monitor how well agents are performing. Transparency of information flows increasingly is becoming the norm—on the principle that citizens always are the ultimate principals—even where the

FIGURE 1.1 National Governance Systems—Actors and Accountabilities

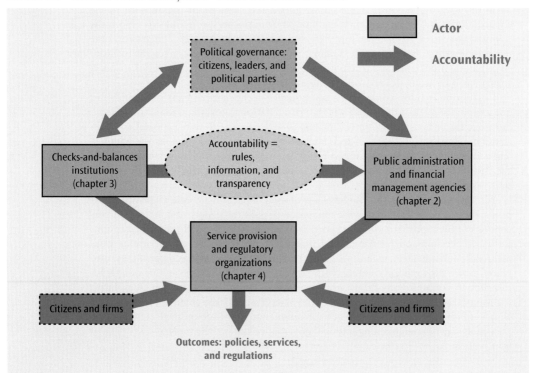

Source: Author.

immediate principal-agent relationship might be between different parts of the state. As table 1.1 highlights, transparency's role potentially is pervasive—from the political apex of a national governance system all the way to the service provision front line—creating plentiful opportunities for engagement.

■ Enforcement mechanisms that reward successful performance and sanction those who fail to perform well.

Development outcomes depend on the operation of the national governance system as a whole. Sustained good results imply that the capacities of the players and the accountabilities among them are strong.

Turning to the five sets of actors identified in figure 1.1, the first comprises citizens, leaders, and political parties in the political governance subsystem—that is, the mechanisms for citizens to select their political leaders at national and subnational levels, and the ways organized groups of citizens influence politics and government.

Politics is the prime influence on governance. Political leaders set the objectives for the rest of the governance system. Sometimes politicians work to address the general interest. Other times, their behavior is clientelistic, in the sense that "even

TABLE 1.1 Nodes of Transparency in National Governance Systems

Node-specific examples of transparency	
Node 1: Transparency in political governance	• Disclosure by political candidates and public officials of assets, education, and criminal record • Widely available public information on the performance of government
Node 2: Transparency in public administration and financial management	• Open competitive system of public procurement • Meritocratic recruitment of public sector employees • Transparent in-year financial reporting
Node 3: Transparent oversight of public administration by checks-and-balances institutions	• Participatory budget formulation process, including cabinet-level and parliamentary discussions • Timely, comprehensive, high quality, and publicly available audit of budget by independent institutions
Node 4: Checks-and-balances institutions ensure open flow of information	• Free press • Freedom of information act • Publication of judicial and administrative decisions • Open decision-making processes • Publication of parliamentary debates
Node 5: Transparency in relationship between citizens/firms and service providers	• Independent service delivery scorecards/surveys • Public information on results by provider organizations (monitoring and evaluation data, annual reports, and so on) • Service charters issued by provider organizations • Publicly posted information on financial and other resources provided to provider organizations

Source: Authors.

though the average citizen is poor, politicians...shift public spending to cater to special interests, to core supporters, or to 'swing' voters."[8] What shapes whether politicians behave in developmental rather than clientelistic ways? Only rarely can they decide themselves—usually they are constrained by having to maintain their support base. Skillful, farsighted politicians, especially those at the head of political movements rooted in a broad social vision, may be able to shape the objectives for their supporters. But the process is often driven more by responding to the interests of key allies, and sometimes these powerful interests may capture the state. Note that, as box 1.3 details, even a democratic electoral process does not guarantee that politicians will focus on the general interest. Note that the general interest can also guide the actions of some politicians in nondemocratic societies.

A second set of actors consists of checks-and-balances institutions, including parliaments, independent oversight agencies (supreme audit institutions, ombudsmen, anticorruption commissions), the judicial system, a free press, and democratically accountable local institutions. These institutions have at least three distinct functions. They establish the rules of the game for political competition. They provide the rules of the game for the broader working of civil society and for the operation of the private market economy. And they limit the influence of politicians on the bureaucracy. Checks-and-balances institutions are a ubiquitous feature of polities—not only of liberal democracies—though their specific forms can vary with the mode of political organization. Checks-and balances-institutions are the subject of chapter 3.

The third set of actors (considered in chapter 2) comprises the cross-cutting control agencies responsible for public administration and financial management, including those responsible for budget formulation, execution, and reporting systems; procurement systems; monitoring and evaluation systems; intergovernmental systems; and civil service management systems.

The fourth set (examined in chapter 4) includes service provision and regulatory organizations, including sectoral line ministries, autonomous public or private front-line providers, and regulatory agencies. These two sets of players make up the public bureaucracy, which follows objectives established by political leaders within a framework set by checks-and-balances institutions. Within the bureaucracy, cross-cutting bureaucratic control agencies oversee service provision and regulatory agencies. This is where options for prioritization and resource allocation are developed, and where the responsibility lies for establishing and enforcing the rules and accountabilities (for example, the financial management and personnel rules) within which service provider and regulatory agencies operate. The justice system plays a dual role, as a checks-and-balances institution and as a provider of dispute-resolution services to society.

The fifth set of actors comprises citizens and firms as users of public services, including regulatory services and service providers. Citizens and firms can be depicted as principals, holding providers (agents) accountable for the efficiency and effectiveness of service provision. The extent to which they can do this depends on the quality and transparency of information flows. In markets with both public and private providers, competition can be a powerful disciplining influence on all providers, including those in the public sector.

To illustrate the relevance of the framework, one might consider two very different configurations along a spectrum of governance quality. The first pattern—

BOX 1.3 How Information Links Democracy and Development Effectiveness

Elections are a peaceful and seemingly low-cost way of enabling citizens to exercise influence over the selection of government leaders. One might expect that countries that provide an electoral means for citizens to remove leaders from office who do not perform in the general interest would perform better than countries that do not, with less corruption and better service provision. However, though it is well known that the richest governments with the fewest governance problems are democracies, it turns out that on most policy dimensions, poor democracies seem to perform about the same as poor nondemocracies.

The reason is that the conditions of political competition, beyond competitive elections, matter greatly in the ability of citizens to hold governments accountable. Two aspects seem key: the ability of political competitors to make credible promises to citizens, and the ability of voters to observe political actions and how those actions affect their welfare. In the absence of either (and they are related, since credible promises are impossible without a means of verifying them), political challengers are unable to promise that they will do better than poorly performing incumbents, insulating incumbents from pressure.

Evidence for these propositions is significant and growing. With respect to information, as detailed further in Box 3.8, newspaper circulation and access to radio have been found to cause lower corruption and better access to government transfers. The local publication of capitation grants from the Ugandan central government to schools led to a dramatic reduction in leakage.

With respect to credibility, evidence is less direct. However, those democracies in which political competitors are likely to be least able to make credible promises are those that have been in existence fewer years. In fact, the policies pursued by young and older democracies with respect to corruption, public investment, public sector wages, government ownership of newspapers, bureaucratic quality, and the rule of law, differ in precisely the ways that we would expect if politicians in younger democracies were unable to make credible promises.

These diagnoses help us to formulate policies for attacking the systemic roots of poor governance. In particular, as the governance discussion in this publication emphasizes throughout, information strategies that help citizens understand what politicians have done and how those actions affect them are both powerful and easily doable. These can be at the project level, such as when donors publicize the results of monitoring and evaluation studies; at the sectoral level, where governments collect and disseminate information about expenditures and outcomes; or at the policy level, where reforms are undertaken to laws that obstruct citizen access to information, such as controls on media ownership, censorship, and prohibitions on citizen access to government information.

Sources: Keefer and Khemani 2005, 1–27; Keefer 2005.

sometimes termed *good enough governance*—summarizes the attributes of consistently stronger governance.[9] For governance to be good enough, the public bureaucracy need not perform at the highest levels of efficiency. More important is that the accountability arrangements built into the national governance system be mutually reinforcing, so that the system can self-correct. Failure in one part of the system (such as corruption in the use of public funds) generates pressures from other parts (parliament, courts, or citizen groups) to refocus on the public purpose.

The contrasting pattern—*clientelist governance*—characterizes countries with much weaker governance performance. In clientelist countries, formal and informal systems of authority work at cross-purposes, and the latter dominates the former.[10] Political leaders use their control over patronage resources to maintain their power base; at the limit, they are captured by powerful private interests. Leaders can bypass or override checks-and-balances institutions and the public administration when these get in the way of their political goals. Systems are not transparent. Levels of corruption are generally high. Informal norms are, of course, also a reality in better-governed settings; however, they do not conflict as egregiously with the formal arrangements.

Clientelist systems may limit development, but they can be stable if political leaders choose to exercise sufficient restraint to enable the formal system to operate, however imperfectly. This is more likely when they take a long-term view and recognize the importance of sustaining the institutional capacity to govern. The result—as observed in Africa in the 1970s and 1980s, for example—may be a seemingly long-term clientelist equilibrium. But this equilibrium can turn into an accelerating downward spiral if the time horizon of leaders is short. Bureaucratic decay deepens as organizations lose resources and competent staff. Economic decay deepens as public services weaken and policy becomes more capricious. Investor confidence evaporates and political decay deepens as the leadership finds itself trying to buy off constituencies with fewer and fewer resources. At the limit (as in Sierra Leone) the endpoint of this downward spiral of decay can be the collapse of the state.

For many low-income countries, improving governance means breaking out of the trap of clientelism. Because clientelism (like all governance arrangements) is deeply intertwined with the structure and exercise of political power, this can be enormously difficult. Different societies find different ways to break free. As a result, their trajectories of governance reform vary—with corresponding differences across countries as to which actors and accountabilities improve rapidly, and which lag. As will become evident, these variations have important implications for both governance monitoring and reform.

Indicators of Governance

Even with greater clarity about the relevant institutions, measuring their quality is difficult. Formal systems can be categorized and rated, but the gap between formal arrangements and realities on the ground is often very wide. Institutional processes are difficult to observe and measure systematically. Some outcomes can be measured, but these can have multiple causes and are often remote from the quality of governance. There are ways of responding to these measurement difficulties, but all are imperfect—and often subject to large margins of error.

The framework suggests two distinct approaches to monitoring the quality of governance. The first is to monitor at a disaggregated level, using specific measures of the quality of key governance subsystems, and to use the results as "actionable indicators" to identify specific strengths and weaknesses in individual countries, and thus to guide reforms and track progress. The second is to monitor governance at more aggregate levels, using broad measures. Broad measures have different uses from their specific counterparts. They can help reveal some systematic patterns underlying the complexity and diversity across individual subsystems, and they can provide some basis for monitoring overall trends across countries and over time.

Broad measures of governance can be derived in two ways. First, they can be composite measures built up from disaggregated indicators. Sometimes, such measures are constructed in a way that makes it possible to drill down from aggregated to disaggregated levels, and thereby identify strengths and weaknesses in an action-oriented way. In practice, governance measurement has not yet advanced to the point that this is routinely feasible, despite some advances in this direction. Second, broad indicators could be derived by focusing on the outcomes produced by national governance systems.

This report reviews and applies both broad and specific governance indicators. Irrespective of the level of aggregation, few governance data sets are objectively measurable indicators; multiple attempts reveal how difficult it is to construct them.[11] The data mostly reflect subjective perceptions—sometimes expert assessments, other times survey-based measures of the perception of citizens or firms. Some surveys, however, do ask questions that produce "objective" data—for example, the share of household income or sales revenues used to pay bribes. While the use of expert assessments and perception-based data is ubiquitous in the social sciences, caution—and careful attention to the likely margins of uncertainty—is needed in the interpretation of results. Indeed, as the next sections will illustrate, some measurement error is inevitable, regardless of the type of measure used.

The Variety

Few of the 33 data sources listed in *Governance Indicators: A Users' Guide* (UNDP 2004), can be used straightforwardly in this report. Some fall short of the requisite comprehensiveness of country coverage—particularly those of low-income countries. Others are collected irregularly, weakening their ability to measure trends. This report focuses on a subset of 14 measures that offer comprehensive country coverage and, between them, cover each of the diverse facets of national governance systems in the framework. (See table 1.5 at the end of this chapter). Three sets of indicators—the World Bank's CPIAs, which account for 5 of the 14 indicators; the Kaufmann-Kraay aggregate governance indicators, which account for 3 additional indicators; and 3 selected indicators from the DB database and the ICSs—are examined in this chapter. Other indicators are examined in chapters 2 through 4.

The CPIA

In the late 1970s, the World Bank began using systematic country assessments to guide the allocation of IDA resources. By the late 1990s, the CPIA had evolved to something close to its current format. A further round of fine-tuning came in 2004, to implement suggestions by an independent panel of outside experts. The 2005 CPIAs are the first publicly available detailed scores for IDA countries.

CPIAs examine policies and institutions, not development outcomes, which can depend on forces outside a country's control. The CPIA looks at 16 distinct areas grouped into four clusters (box 1.4). For each criterion, very detailed guidelines are provided to help Bank staff score individual countries along an absolute 1–6 scale.

For monitoring governance systems, the CPIA indicators can be used in three ways:

- At the most disaggregate level, scores for individual criteria in the public sector management and institutions cluster can be quite specific and actionable. The analysis of public budget and administrative management systems in the next chapter will draw on CPIA criteria 13 and 15.
- The average score for the public sector management and institutions cluster (cluster D) can be an aggregate indicator of the quality of a country's governance system. Table 1.2 places 66 low-income, potential IDA-recipient countries into five groups, according to their CPIA cluster D scores for 2004.[12]
- The average score for clusters A, B, and C can be an aggregate measure of the quality of a country's economic and sectoral policies—viewed as an outcome measure of the quality of a country's governance system.

BOX 1.4 The 2004 CPIA's 16 criteria

A. **Economic management**
  1. Macroeconomic management
  2. Fiscal policy
  3. Debt policy

B. **Structural policies**
  4. Trade
  5. Financial sector
  6. Business regulatory environment

C. **Policies for social inclusion/equity**
  7. Gender equality
  8. Equity of public resource use
  9. Building human resources
  10. Social protection and labor
  11. Policies and institutions for environmental sustainability

D. **Public sector management and institutions**
  12. Property rights and rule-based governance
  13. Quality of budgetary and financial management
  14. Efficiency of revenue mobilization
  15. Quality of public administration
  16. Transparency, accountability, and corruption in the public sector

---

As with all indicators, the CPIA has its limitations. The assessments are made by World Bank staff. Even if expert in their field and well informed about individual countries, staff sometimes may not be aware of the intimate details of how things really work in a country. Some of the criteria do not readily lend themselves to an ordinal scale of quality—even though "the criteria were developed to ensure that, to the extent possible, their contents are developmental neutral, that the higher scores do not set unduly demanding standards, and can be attained by a country that, given its stage of development, has a policy and institutional framework that strongly fosters growth and poverty reduction."[13] Policy expectations in some areas, such as social protection, are different for low- and higher-income countries. Staff assessments can be affected by the fact that the CPIA forms the basis for allocating IDA resources. There are risks of ideological bias—for example, on the merits of low tariffs versus an export-neutral combination of tariffs and subsidies. To address these limitations and assure consistency across countries, the World Bank goes through an elaborate, multistage process for scoring the CPIAs. The process includes: an initial round of benchmarking by a global team drawn from across the World Bank; subsequent rounds within operating regions using the benchmarked countries as guideposts; and a further round of validation by central units. The results are discussed with national governments, but final scoring rests with the Bank.

Given the above, it is appropriate to interpret CPIA scores as estimates, with some margin of error. Estimates place the standard error at about 0.24 for aggregate measures on the 1–6 scale (see box 1.5). Ultimately, open debate offers the best way of uncovering and addressing remaining weaknesses in the CPIA. The decision to make public the detailed 2005 CPIA scores for IDA-recipient countries is an

TABLE 1.2   2004 Country Scores for the CPIA Public Institutions Cluster

CPIA institutions cluster score	Countries
Above 3.5	Armenia, Bhutan, Ghana, India, Mali, Senegal, Tanzania
3.3–3.5	Benin, Bosnia and Herzegovina, Burkina Faso, Ethiopia, Georgia, Honduras, Indonesia, Kenya, Lesotho, Madagascar, Malawi, Nicaragua, Pakistan, Rwanda, Serbia and Montenegro, Sri Lanka, Uganda, Vietnam
3.0–3.2	Albania, Azerbaijan, Bangladesh, Bolivia, Cameroon, Eritrea, Guyana, Moldova, Mauritania, Mongolia, Mozambique, Nepal, Niger, Papua New Guinea, São Tomé and Principe, Zambia
2.6–2.9	Burundi, Chad, Congo, Rep. of, Côte d'Ivoire, Djibouti, Gambia, The, Guinea, Kyrgyz Republic, Nigeria, Sierra Leone, Solomon Islands, Tajikistan, Uzbekistan, Yemen, Republic of
2.5 or below	Angola, Comoros, Central African Republic, Congo, Dem. Rep. of, Guinea-Bissau, Lao PDR, Sudan, Togo

Source: World Bank.

important step in the ongoing process of enhancing the transparency of this potentially important indicator.

Kaufmann-Kraay

The Kaufmann-Kraay (KK) indicators, published on the Web site of the World Bank Institute, are the product of research conducted by World Bank staff. But unlike the CPIAs, they are not a formal World Bank product, and they are not used in any systematic way in World Bank decisions. They are one response to the problem of aggregation. They generate a set of six composite aggregate indicators from a proliferation of loosely connected disaggregated measures by using a technique for sta-

---

BOX 1.5   How Precise Is the CPIA?

Any rating system is bound to be subject to some error, and the CPIA is no exception. Estimating the error requires a number of independent assessments using the same rating system. This is not possible. But comparisons of the overall scores for the World Bank's ratings and the independent ratings of the African Development Bank, which uses a similar system, offers a quasi-experimental opportunity. As the figure here shows, the ratings are strongly correlated.

BOX FIGURE A1 CPIA Distributions, 1999–2002

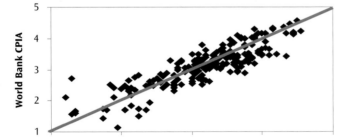

Scatter graph of AfDB and WB CPIA, 1999–2002

Sources: African Development Bank and World Bank.

Subject to some assumptions (see Gelb, Ngo, and Ye 2004), this comparison yields an estimate of the standard error of a CPIA rating of 0.24 points on the scale of 1–6, with comparable standard error estimates for the four individual clusters of questions. Analysts are therefore generally able to distinguish well-performing countries (rating of 4 plus) from middle performers (rating of 3.5), and are clearly able to distinguish them from low performers (3.0 or below). But within each category there can be considerable uncertainty over the shading of performance.

BOX 1.5 How Precise Is the CPIA? (continued)

The error estimate also indicates the need for caution in using CPIA-type assessments to measure trends in performance over short periods when the change in an overall rating—typically around plus or minus 0.1 points over a year—can be smaller than the standard error of the estimate. Year-on-year changes in the two CPIA estimates may therefore not be highly correlated. But changes over several years tend to move in the same direction. For example, for the period 1999–2004, the correlation between the average change in the two ratings is 0.83, and in all but eight of the 51 countries, the changes move in the same direction.

Scatter graph of AfDB and WB CPIA averages of 1-year changes, 1999–2004

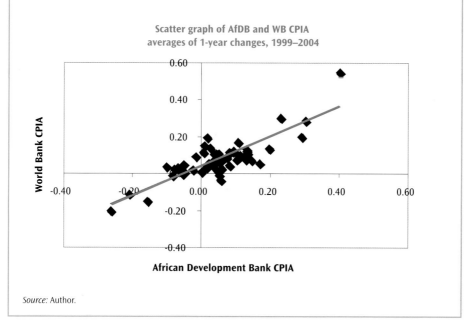

Source: Author.

tistical aggregation, the unobserved components model. The six aggregate governance indicators are as follows:

- Voice and accountability
- Political stability and absence of violence
- Government effectiveness
- Regulatory quality
- Rule of law
- Control of corruption

These indicators, available for every second year from 1996 to 2004, are an amalgam of 352 variables, culled from 37 data sources produced by 31 organizations. Three of these indicators—voice and accountability, rule of law, and control of corruption—will be used as part of governance monitoring in this and the next chapter.

Kaufmann and Kraay explain the aggregation approach as follows: "The prem-ise [is that] each of the individual data sources provides an imperfect signal of some deep underlying notion of governance that is difficult to observe directly...that, within each cluster, each of these indicators measures a similar underlying basic concept of governance...[The challenge is to] isolate the informative signal about governance from each data source, and to optimally combine the many data sources to get the best possible signal of governance in a country based on all the available data...The unobserved components model expresses the observed data in each clus-ter as a linear function of the unobserved common component of governance, plus a disturbance term capturing perception errors and/or sampling variation in each indicator."[14]

The aggregation procedure used by KK has some important strengths for empir-ical work on governance. The methodology enables very broad country and terri-tory coverage. The aggregation procedure generates, for each country, both point estimates and standard errors of these estimates.

By making explicit the standard errors of their estimates, the KK measures high-light how challenging it is to precisely measure the quality of governance, both for broad and for specific measures. Specific measures often are based on sample sur-veys or on expert assessments, with the risk of sampling error in the former (although robust sampling and statistical methodologies can reduce the range of error), and of informant error in the latter (although robust peer review can limit this risk). By combining multiple sources into a single measure, KK helps reduce uncertainty of this type; their approach takes advantage of the well-known statis-tical property that the margin of error of a measure declines as the number of inde-pendently generated estimates increases.

The cost, though, is to introduce a different type of uncertainty. KK's gain in pre-cision is offset by a loss of *specificity*. The KK composite variables combine sources that measure similar, but not identical, phenomena. A country's poor score on one of the aggregate indicators might reflect divergent performance among the under-lying sources, making the indicators less useful as actionable tools. Further, the KK methodology both presumes that each of its sources is independently generated, and weights converging sources more heavily. But if in fact the converging sources draw on a shared underlying model, the methodology risks marginalizing sources that offer a view that is different, but not necessarily wrong.[15]

The example of corruption illustrates the use and limitations of aggregate indi-cators. Two sets of aggregate indicators—the KK "control of corruption" aggre-gate indicator, and Transparency International's (TI) Corruptions Perceptions Index[16]—provide "best practice" aggregate indicators, and so have dominated cross-country ratings of corruption. Both rank countries according to their per-ceived performance in controlling corruption, and both report margins of error of their estimates; the country estimates for both are included in the statistical annex. Each indicator draws on multiple primary indicators to produce country rankings. The KK indicator description indicates what is being measured, namely:

> *...perceptions of corruption, conventionally defined as the exercise of public power for private gain. The particular aspect of corruption ranges from the frequency of "additional payments to get things done" to the effects of cor-*

*ruption on the business environment, to measuring "grand corruption" in the
political arena or in the tendency of elites to engage in "state capture…"*

Although the KK and TI methodologies differ,[17] in practice their results are very
similar, with a correlation coefficient of 0.97. Either indicator can be used for comparisons across countries and over time. Table 1.3 summarizes the 2004 KK corruption results by grouping 204 countries into three categories by their extent of
corruption, distinguishing among countries according to whether one can be at
least 95 percent confident, using a two-tailed test, that given measurement errors,
they indeed fall into the category in which they are located, and separating, for pre-
sentational simplicity, OECD and middle- and high-income countries from countries eligible for IDA.[18] Within the latter group, countries falling into the bottom
quintile of the global ranking are identified. The country names are in annex table
1.1. Two conclusions:

- Middle- and high-income countries are usually in the least corrupt third of countries, and low-income, IDA-recipient countries in the most corrupt third. This
  distribution reflects the well-known inverse correlation between per-capita
  income and levels of corruption. But even within the general pattern, levels of
  corruption vary widely for countries at similar levels of per-capita income—
  implying that corruption is not wholly tied to income.
- It is possible to position countries on a global corruption spectrum only in broad
  terms. Only for 84 of the 204 countries in the table—and only for 36 of the 70
  countries in the bottom third—can one have at least 95 percent confidence that they
  belong in the third in which they have been placed. Only nine countries can be
  clearly identified as being in the weakest quintile of the global distribution. Given
  the wide margins of error, it is misleading to emphasize precise country rankings.

Doing Business and the Investment Climate Surveys

The World Bank-sponsored DB and ICS surveys are designed to monitor the business environment, not governance. Some of the business environment measures can
nonetheless be directly linked to governance, and therefore are useful for governance monitoring.

The DB and ICS methodologies are very different. The ICS captures business perceptions on the biggest obstacles to enterprise growth, the relative importance of various constraints to increasing employment and productivity, and the effects of a
country's investment climate on its international competitiveness. DB indicators comprise detailed, objective measures of the time and cost of strict compliance with government regulations affecting private business across 10 topic areas—the number of
procedures required to accomplish the task in question, the number of days necessary
to accomplish the task, and the monetary cost in required fees. Input and verification
are provided by government officials, lawyers, business consultants, accountants, and
other professionals administering or advising on regulatory requirements.

Both the DB and ICS indicators are, of course, subject to measurement error.
Their differing methodologies have different strengths and weaknesses, making
them usefully complementary to one another:

TABLE 1.3   KK Estimates of the Extent of Corruption in 204 Countries, 2004

High- and middle-income economies (excluding blends; including IDA eligible-island-MICs)

	With 95% certainty in relevant row	With less than 95% certainty in relevant row	
Top Third	21 Plus 23 OECD	18 Plus 2 OECD	
Middle Third	11 Plus 2 OECD	Could be in bottom third: 14	Could be in top third: 20 Plus 3 OECD
Bottom Third	8	9	

IDA and blend countries (excluding IDA eligible island MICs)

	With 95% certainty in relevant row	With less than 95% certainty in relevant row	
Top Third		1	
Middle Third	5	Could be in bottom third: 13	Could be in top third: 1
Bottom Third [21–33 percent]	5	With 95 % certainty in bottom half: 17	3
Bottom 20 percent	9	With 95 % certainty in bottom third: 14	With 95 % certainty in bottom half: 5

Source: Kaufmann, Kraay, and Mastruzzi 2005.
For data notes see annex table 1.1.

- ■ *De jure versus de facto:* The DB product measures the de jure business environment, whereas the ICS product measures the de facto business environment. Both measures are useful, although it is important not to confuse changes in the de jure environment with actual changes on the ground.[19]
- ■ *In-depth versus holistic perspective:* The DB product zeroes in on a narrow set of transactions which it presumes to be illustrative of the business environment more broadly, whereas the ICS product provides a holistic view of the business environment from the perspective of firms themselves.
- ■ *Cost and coverage:* DB covers 155 countries, and all country scores are updated annually. The ICS is a more effort-intensive product. Its database contains information on about 75 countries; it aims to cover 20 to 30 countries each year and resurvey each country every three years or so. High costs somewhat limit the ICS' usefulness as a tool for ongoing governance measurement across a large number of countries.

A first potential use of these business environment indicators for governance monitoring is as overall outcome measures, complementing the CPIA and KK. Box 1.6 highlights three specific measures that can play this role: the ICS measures of corruption, plus two measures of transactions costs associated with bureaucratic red tape. (Annex table 1.2 lists additional ICS and DB measures that are useful for monitoring corruption and bureaucratic red tape.) Irrespective of how much business regulation a country judges to be appropriate, it always is developmentally desirable to minimize the time and hassle spent in complying. In general, high transactions costs signal some combination of an unresponsive bureaucracy, or a clientelistic environment geared to providing opportunities for informal rent extraction by public officials.

A second potential use of the ICS data in particular is to distinguish among different types of corruption. Corruption sometimes is disaggregated into two basic forms—*state capture and administrative corruption*. State capture refers to the actions of individuals, groups, or firms in either the public or private sectors to influence the *formulation* of laws, regulations, decrees, and other government policies to their own advantage as a result of the illicit and nontransparent provision of benefits to public officials. State capture is commonly found in states that control important national assets, either through ownership (for instance, mineral rights, state-owned enterprises) or regulation (for instance, economic or environmental), but have limited political competition and weaker checks and balances. Administrative corruption refers to the provision of illicit and nontransparent benefits to influence how these established rules are *implemented*. Administrative corruption flourishes in states with weaker bureaucratic capacity and accountability. The ICS surveys conducted in Eastern and Southeastern Europe and the former

---

BOX 1.6 Three Aggregate Governance Doing Business and Investment Climate Survey Indicators

Unofficial payments for firms to get things done (percentage of sales) (ICS)
Average value of gifts or informal payments to public officials to "get things done" with regard to customs, taxes, licenses, regulations, services, and the like. The values shown indicate a percentage of annual sales.

Dealing with licenses (DB)
The number of procedures, average time spent during each procedure, and official cost of each procedure involved in obtaining necessary licenses and permits, completing required notifications and inspections, and obtaining utility connections (using construction of a warehouse as a benchmark example).

Senior management time spent dealing with requirements of regulations (percentage) (ICS)
Average percentage of senior management's time that is spent in a typical week dealing with requirements imposed by government regulations (such as taxes, customs, labor regulations, licensing, and registration), including dealings with officials, completing forms, and the like.

Soviet Union (known as the BEEPS surveys)[20] framed their questions in a way that made it possible to distinguish between the different types of corruption. The surveys found that the relative balance between state capture and administrative corruption can vary widely from country to country.

A third use of the DB and ICS data is to measure trends over time for specific features of the governance environment within specific countries. Where survey

FIGURE 1.2 Trends in Administrative Corruption in Europe

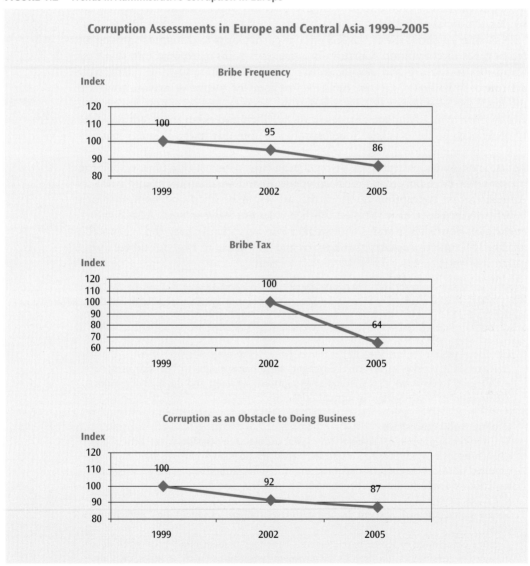

Corruption Assessments in Europe and Central Asia 1999–2005

Sources: The World Bank and the EBRD Business Environment and Enterprise Surveys (BEEPS) 1999, 2002, 2005.
Note: The charts depict 2002 and 2005 values relative to 1999, except in the case of bribe tax, where the 2005 value is shown relative to 2002. Due to a change in wording, the bribe tax is not comparable between 1999 and 2002. Values are based on the simple average of country means over all countries that were present in all years.

variables are narrowly defined, and the sampling and statistical work are careful, the resulting measures can have small margins of error, and so make evident incremental changes over time. Figure 1.2 draws on the 1999, 2002, and 2005 BEEPS surveys to report trends in administrative corruption for the 26 surveyed countries. The figure points to broad declines in administrative corruption—an important success, and one that needs careful and sustained survey analysis such as that done by BEEPS to assure that the evidence of positive—encouraging and, to some, surprising—trends such as this one is indeed persuasive.[21]

Finally, the DB and ICS data also are useful as specific, disaggregated measures of the performance of individual public service provision or regulatory agencies or sectors. Along with measures of corruption and bureaucratic red tape, annex table 1.2 highlights two additional categories of specific DB and ICS measures that are useful for governance monitoring: measures of the quality of provision of education, water, and telecommunications services; and measures of the quality of justice and the rule of law. Figure 1.3 illustrates the products' usefulness with data (again for the 26 BEEPS countries) on variations across sectors in the incidence of corruption.

Governance Monitoring—from Broad to Specific

Ten years ago, the TI, KK, and DB indexes did not exist, the CPIA was still quite rudimentary, and none of it was public. The ICS was not being done on a systematic basis globally. Over the past decade, there have thus been major advances in the development of broad indicators for monitoring governance.

Combining different indexes yields some striking patterns, additional to those described above. Table 1.4 combines the country results for two sets of broad outcome indicators—the KK control of corruption measure, and the quality of a country's economic and sectoral policies (as measured by the average score for CPIA clusters A, B, and C).[22] Three key lessons emerge.

First, the broad indicators offer a first approximation of the patterns of variation in governance performance among 66 IDA recipient countries. About one-third of countries generally are in

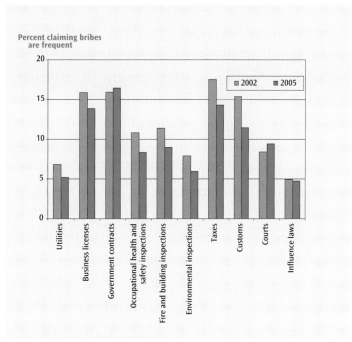

FIGURE 1.3   Corruption in Specific Sectors in ECA, 2002–05

Sources: World Bank and EBRD 2002 and 2005.
Note: The chart depicts the simple mean of the country averages of the percent of firms that said bribes were frequent.

the higher "good enough" quintiles of both broad governance outcome indicators. Another third are lodged firmly in the lower "clientelistic" quintiles of the indicator sets.[23]

Second, these consistent clusters aside, what is especially striking is the uneven mix of strengths and weaknesses for individual countries. Country performance is broadly similar on both dimensions for 34 of the 66 IDA-eligible countries. But (even making substantial allowance for the margins of error in measurement) in 17 countries the quality of policy and institutions is better than performance on corruption, and 15 countries show the opposite pattern. Bangladesh currently is perhaps the best-known example of a country with relatively weak perceived control of corruption but strong performance on policies and on poverty reduction—though, as table 1.3 suggests, many other countries evince a similar pattern.

Countries can thus differ. Some with weak policies appear to be less corrupt. And others, stronger on the policy front, seem less successful in controlling corruption. This divergence raises some questions, both for governance monitoring and more broadly:

- If the divergence is not simply the result of measurement error (and the allowance for large margins of error in the construction of table 1.4 suggests that it mostly is not), is it pointing to some underlying structural or social features, or to differences across countries in the relative importance ascribed to good policy on the one hand, and the fight against corruption on the other?
- How do differences in the relative importance ascribed to these different dimensions affect country performance on poverty reduction?
- How should donors respond to this divergence? Should they differentiate their support as between countries that fight corruption determinedly but have relatively weak policy, and countries stronger on the policy front than on reining in corruption?
- How do such differences reflect the performance of specific governance subsystems? Which are most relevant for containing corruption?

The third lesson follows from the fact that indicators (both broad and specific) generally have large errors. Quantifying these margins of error has been an important advance over the past decade. The consensus among researchers is that, by and large, the broad governance indicators we have are what we will have to work with—no breakthrough capable of providing an overarching, yet precise measure of governance is on the horizon. This signals the limitations of efforts to classify countries according to their broad governance performance. Further, country-focused operational work also requires indicators that are specific, and identify "actionable" entry points for reform

Governance monitoring thus needs to make balanced use of both broad and more specific indicators. The GMR (and so this paper) identifies 14 indicators—all of which are italicized in table 1.5—both broad and specific, as core for governance monitoring. (The CPIA, KK, DB, and ICS indicators have already been introduced; the others will be introduced in chapters 2 and 3.) Most come from sources that are updated every year or two, such as the CPIA, KK, and TI. Country coverage already is comprehensive for these and for DB and Polity IV; many countries are also being included

TABLE 1.4   Intermediate Outcomes—Corruption Versus Policy

Relative performance across governance outcomes	CPIA 2004 policy quintiles (cluster (a)–(c) average)				
	Bottom quintile	4th quintile	3rd quintile	2nd quintile	Top quintile
Control of corruption and policy performance are broadly similar[a]	Angola, Central African Republic, Comoros, Congo, Dem. Rep. of, Côte d'Ivoire, Lao PDR, Nigeria, Solomon Islands, Sudan	Burundi, Cambodia, Congo, Rep. of, Djibouti, Papua New Guinea, Sierra Leone, Zambia	Cameroon, Ethiopia, Kenya, Malawi, Moldova, Nepal, Rwanda, Mozambique, Rep. of Yemen, Niger	Benin, Bosnia and Herzegovina, Mali, Serbia and Montenegro, Sri Lanka	Burkina Faso, Nicaragua, Senegal
Better policies, weaker control of corruption[b]		Chad, Haiti, Uzbekistan	Tajikistan	Bangladesh, Georgia, Kyrgyz Republic, Indonesia, Vietnam	Albania, Armenia, Azerbaijan, Bolivia, Honduras, Pakistan, Tanzania, Uganda
Better corruption control, less good policies[c]	Eritrea, Guinea-Bissau, São Tomé and Principe, Togo, Zimbabwe	The Gambia, Guinea, Mauritania	Mongolia, Lesotho	Bhutan, Ghana, Guyana, India, Madagascar	

Source: World Bank CPIA Database.
a. Country percentile rank for the CPIA Policy Outcome and the Kaufmann, Kraay, and Zoido-Lobaton (KKZ) Control of Corruption indicator are less than 20 percentile points apart.
b. Country percentile rank for Policy Outcome is better than Control of Corruption by percentile rank of at least 20 points.
c. Country percentile rank for Control of Corruption is better than Policy Outcome by percentile rank of at least 20 points.

in periodic ICS. The exception is the PEFA indicator set, developed by the Public Expenditure and Financial Accountability global program. Effective monitoring of the quality of public financial management is central to the new approach for scaling up aid. *The GMR thus recommends that priority attention be given to more systematically applying the PEFA indicators in all major aid-recipient countries.*

Along with the 14 core indicators, table 1.5 also identifies a variety of other (nonitalicized) indicators that are useful for global monitoring. All of these are specific actionable indicators. Of the specific indicators, the DB, ICS, and Statistical Capacity indexes already are available comprehensively—using the others for monitoring remains a work in progress. The Global Integrity index was applied in an initial 25 countries in 2004, and in 43 countries in 2006 (of which 15 were repeats). The procurement index, the OECD-DAC (Development Assistance Committee) Baseline Indicator Set (BIS) for Procurement—has been proposed to be piloted in 10 countries. Specific actionable indicators measuring key aspects of public administration have been piloted in three countries. The number of service-provision-specific indicators potentially is large, though so far only one that is clearly governance

TABLE 1.5   Governance Monitoring Indicators

	Indicators with comprehensive country coverage	Other key indicators
Overall governance performance	*1, 2, 3. Control of corruption* (KK, TI, ICS) *4. Policy outcome* (CPIA cluster a–c average) *5. Aggregate public institutions* (CPIA cluster d) *6, 7. Business transactions costs* (DB, ICS)	
Bureaucratic capability	*8. Budget/financial management* (CPIA-budget) *9. Public administration* (CPIA-admin) Doing Business indicators Investment Climate Surveys Statistical Capacity	*14. PEFA indicators* Procurement "Actionable" public administration Service-provision-specific
Checks-and-balances institutions	*10. Voice and accountability* (KK) *11, 12. Justice and rule of law* (KK, CPIA-rules) *13. Executive constraints* (Polity IV)	Global Integrity Index

Source: Authors.
Note: Each indicator set is described in the text; the 14 italicized indicators are considered key by the GMR.

related—teacher absenteeism—has been collected systematically, and so far for fewer than a dozen countries. Although the cost of developing and applying these indicators across a large number of countries is high, the PEFA, DB, and ICS experiences suggest that the benefits can be higher still. *The GMR recommends that support be given for the further development of actionable indicators.*

Work on these specific indicators is emerging as the frontier challenge for governance monitoring. They focus on a narrow target for measurement, so if the indicators are carefully defined, and the methodologies for measurement robust, specific measures can provide tighter margins of error, even if they cannot easily be used as proxies for broader governance outcomes. The narrow focus of specific measures also makes them actionable in the sense that they can help identify specific governance weaknesses and monitor progress of efforts to address these weaknesses. The next three chapters will focus on monitoring and reform of specific governance subsystems, highlighting the potential uses, both for monitoring and for governance reform, of narrowly focused, actionable indicators.

ANNEX TABLE 1.1 KK Estimates of the Extent of Corruption in 204 Countries, 2004

High- and middle-income economies (excluding blends; including IDA-eligible island-MICs)

	With 95% certainty in relevant row	With less than 95% certainty in relevant row	
Top Third	Andorra, Aruba, Bahamas, Bahrain, Botswana, Cayman Islands, Chile, Costa Rica, Cyprus, Estonia, Hong Kong, Israel, Kuwait, Liechtenstein, Macao, Malta, Oman, Singapore, Slovenia, Taiwan, United Arab Emirates (21 economies) **Of which OECD members are:** Australia, Austria, Belgium, Canada, Denmark, Finland, France, Germany, Hungary, Iceland, Ireland, Italy, Japan, Luxemburg, Netherlands, New Zealand, Norway, Portugal, Spain, Sweden, Switzerland, United Kingdom, United States (23 countries)	Anguilla, Antigua and Barbuda, Barbados, Bermuda, French Guiana, Grenada, Guam, Jordan, Lithuania, Martinique, Netherlands Antilles, Puerto Rico, Qatar, Reunión, South Africa, Suriname, Uruguay, Virgin Islands (18 economies) **Of which OECD members are:** Greece, Slovak Republic (2 countries)	
Middle Third	Brazil, Bulgaria, Colombia, Croatia, Egypt, Malaysia, Morocco, Panama, Romania, Thailand, Trinidad and Tobago (11 countries) **Of which OECD members are:** Mexico, Turkey (2 countries)	**Could be in bottom third:** Algeria, Argentina, China, Dominican Republic, El Salvador, Gabon, Iran, Jamaica, Macedonia, FYR, Micronesia, Peru, Philippines, Vanuatu, West Bank (14 economies)	**Could be in top third:** American Samoa, Belize, Brunei, Cape Verde, Cook Islands, Dominica, Fiji, Kiribati, Latvia, Lebanon, Maldives, Mauritius, Namibia, Samoa, Saudi Arabia, Seychelles, St. Kitts and Nevis, St. Lucia, St. Vincent, Tunisia (20 economies) **Of which OECD members are:** Czech Republic, Poland, South Korea (3 countries)
Bottom Third	Belarus, Equatorial Guinea, Iraq, Kazakhstan, Paraguay, Turkmenistan, Ukraine, Venezuela (8 countries)	Cuba, Ecuador, Guatemala, Marshall Islands, Libya, Russian Federation, Swaziland, Syria, Tonga (9 countries)	

(continued)

ANNEX TABLE 1.1   KK Estimates of the Extent of Corruption in 204 Countries, 2004 (continued)

IDA and blend countries (excluding IDA-eligible island MICs)		
	With 95% certainty in relevant row	**With less than 95% certainty in relevant row**
Top Third		Bhutan (1 country)
Middle Third	Ghana, India, Lesotho, Madagascar, Sri Lanka (5 countries)	**Could be in bottom third:** Armenia, Benin, Bosnia and Herzegovina, Burkina Faso, Guyana, Mali, Mongolia, Nicaragua, Rwanda, Senegal, Serbia, Tanzania, East Timor (13 countries) / **Could be in top third:** Mauritania (1 country)
Bottom Third	Angola, Azerbaijan, Georgia, Indonesia, Moldova (5 countries)	**With 95 % certainty in bottom half:** Albania, Bolivia, Cameroon, Djibouti, Ethiopia, Gambia, Guinea, Guinea-Bissau, Honduras, Malawi, Mozambique, Nepal, Liberia, Uganda, Vietnam, Yemen, Republic of, Zambia (17 countries) / Eritrea, São Tomé and Principe, Tuvalu (3 countries)
Bottom 20 percent	Afghanistan, Central African Republic, Congo Dem. Rep., Haiti, Myanmar, North Korea, Somalia, Sudan, Uzbekistan (9 countries)	**With 95 % certainty in bottom third:** Bangladesh, Burundi, Chad, Comoros, Congo Rep. of, Côte d'Ivoire, Kenya, Kyrgyz Republic, Nigeria, Lao PDR, Papua New Guinea, Solomon Islands, Tajikistan, Zimbabwe (14 countries) / **With 95 % certainty in bottom half:** Cambodia, Niger, Pakistan, Sierra Leone, Togo (5 countries)

Note: The only two countries in the sample that are low income but not in the IDA/Blend list are North Korea and Tuvalu. The inactive-IDA countries—Liberia, Myanmar, Somalia, and Sudan—are included under the IDA group.
Source: Kaufmann, Kraay, and Mastruzzi 2005.

ANNEX TABLE 1.2 Doing Business Indicators and Investment Climate Surveys—Some Useful Measures for Governance Monitoring

A: Measures of Corruption (ICS)
1. **Unofficial payments for firms to get things done (% of sales)**
   Average value of gifts or informal payments to public officials to "get things done" with regard to customs, taxes, licenses, regulations, services, etc. The values shown indicate a percentage of annual sales.
2. **Firms expected to give gifts in meetings with tax inspectors (%)**
   Percentage of firms for which a gift was expected in meeting with tax inspector.
3. **Value of gift expected to secure government contract (% of contract)**
   Percentage of contract value expected as a gift to secure government contract.
4. **Corruption a "major or severe" obstacle (% of firms)**
   Percentage of firms that say corruption is a major or severe obstacle to the operation and growth of their business.

B: *Measures of transactions costs associated with bureaucratic red tape*
   (i) Doing Business Indicators
   1. **Starting a business**
      The number of procedures, average time spent during each procedure, and official cost of each procedure involved in incorporating and registering a commercial or industrial firm.
   2. **Dealing with licenses**
      The number of procedures, average time spent during each procedure, and official cost of each procedure involved in obtaining necessary licenses and permits, completing required notifications and inspections, and obtaining utility connections (using construction of a warehouse as a benchmark example).
   3. **Registering property**
      The number of procedures, average time spent during each procedure, and official cost of each procedure involved in registering property, (using as a benchmark example the case of an entrepreneur who wants to purchase land and building in the largest business city—already registered and free of title dispute).
   4. **Trading across borders**
      Number of documents, approvals, signatures or stamps required, and the time and associated cost necessary to comply with all procedural requirements for exporting and importing a standardized cargo of goods.

   (ii) Investment Climate Indicators
   1. **Senior management time spent dealing with requirements of regulations (%)**
      Average percentage of senior management's time that is spent in a typical week dealing with requirements imposed by government regulations (e.g., taxes, customs, labor regulations, licensing, and registration), including dealings with officials, completing forms, etc.
   2. **Time spent in meetings with tax officials (days)**
      Average time firms spent in meetings with tax officials (days).
   3. **Time to claim imports from customs (days)**
      Average number of days that it takes from the time goods arrive in their point of entry (e.g., port, airport) until the time they can be claimed from customs.
   4. **Customs and trade regulations a "major or severe" obstacle (% of firms)**
      Percentage of firms that say customs regulations present major or severe obstacles to the operation and growth of their business.
C: *Measures of quality of provision of specific public services (ICS)*
   5. **Delay in obtaining a connection (days)** [electricity, water, telephone]
      Average actual delay, in days, that firms experience when obtaining a connection, measured from the day the establishment applied to the day they received the service or approval.
   6. **Supply failures and outages (days)** [electricity, water, telephone]
      Average number of days per year the establishment experienced supply failures and outages from the public network.

(continued)

ANNEX TABLE: 1.2   Doing Business Indicators and Investment Climate Surveys—Some Useful Measures for Governance Monitoring (continued)

7. **Value lost to supply failures (% of sales) [electricity, water, telephone]**
Total losses over the course of a year resulting from interruptions in electricity service, as a percentage of sales, including losses due to lost production time from the outage, time needed to reset machines, and production and sales lost due to processes being interrupted.

8. **Supply weaknesses a "major or severe" obstacle (% of firms)) [electricity, water, telephone]**
Percentage of firms that say the shortcomings of the infrastructure present major or severe obstacles to the operation and growth of their business.

D: Measures of justice and the rule of law (ICS, except #1)

1. **Enforcing Contracts (DB)**
The number of procedures involved from the moment a plaintiff files a lawsuit over a payment dispute until actual payment, and the associated time in calendar days,and cost necessary to resolve the dispute.

2. **Confidence in the judiciary system (%)**
Percentage of firms that agree with the statement "I am confident that the judicial system will enforce my contractual and property rights in business disputes."

3. **Dispute resolution time (weeks)**
Average amount of time, in weeks, that it usually takes to resolve an overdue payment.

4. **Legal system a "major or severe" obstacle (% of firms)**
Percentage of firms that say the legal system presents major or severe obstacles to the operation and growth of their business.

5. **Crime, theft and disorder a "major or severe" obstacle (% of firms)**
Percentage of firms that say crime, theft, and disorder present major or severe obstacles to the operation and growth of their business.

Source: Indicators selected by author.

Notes

3. Coups, for example, often entail only changes in the identity of the kleptocratic chief executive, with few or no implications for the property rights of anyone outside the ruler's and ex-ruler's circles of key supporters.

4. Khan (2002) questions the value of the governance-growth studies, claiming that the direction of causation could be mistaken, and that the relationship is identified only by including the industrialized countries and a few East Asian economies where success resulted from heavy state intervention rather than secure property rights.

5. Rajkumar and Swaroop 2002.

6. Svensson 2005, 19–42.

7. Svensson 2005, 19–42, Yang 2005.

8. World Bank 2004a, 80.

9. For a detailed development of the term, good enough governance, see Grindle (2004).

10. For some theoretical and applied analyses of clientelism, see Bratton and Van Der Walle (1998); Carothers (2002); Levy and Kpundeh (2004); Lewis (1996); Migdal (1988); North (1990); Olson (1991); World Bank (2004a).

11. The Public Expenditure and Financial Accountability (PEFA) indicators incorporate a few objective measures of the quality of budget performance.

12. There are a total of 81 countries eligible for IDA in FY06 (excluding Iraq and Kosovo). Ten "small island economy exception" countries are excluded from the sample. Afghanistan and Timor-Leste do not have CPIA scores and are excluded from this sample. Liberia, Somalia, and Myanmar are inactive IDA countries, and do not have recent CPIA scores.

13. World Bank 2004b, 5.

14. Kaufmann, Kraay, and Mastruzzi 2005, 7; Kaufmann, Kraay, and Zoido-Lobaton 1999, 9.

15. Note that, on average, composite variables do not change much with different weighting schemes.

16. For details about this index and annual results for 1995–2005, see www.transparency.org/policy_and_research/surveys_indices/cpi.

17. See, for example, Kaufmann, Kraay, and Mastruzzi (2005), which contrasts the methodologies used by the two indices for calculating standard errors.

18. North Korea and Tuvalu are the only countries in the KK sample which are low income, but not IDA eligible. Liberia, Myanmar, Somalia, and Sudan are IDA inactive, but included under the IDA group.

19. For an interesting analysis of the relation between de jure and de facto measures of the business environment, see Kaufmann, Kraay, and Mastruzzi (2005). The authors find the correlation between de jure and de facto measures to be about 0.4. The gap is larger in countries with higher perceptions of corruption, signaling the power of informality in working around de jure constraints.

20. These surveys were conducted jointly by the World Bank and the European Bank for Reconstruction and Development; they are known as the Business Environment and Enterprise Performance Surveys (BEEPS).

21. Anderson and Gray 2006, 7–19; Gray, Hellman and Ryterman 2004, 16–23.

22. An alternative approach might have been to view corruption not as an outcome, but as a proxy for the overall quality of public institutions. The correlation coefficient between CPIA cluster D and the KK control of corruption measure is 0.76, suggesting that it is indeed quite a good proxy. Consistent with the substantial dispersion evident in table 5.3, the correlation coefficient between KK corruption and the CPIA clusters A–C average is 0.53.

23. The location of countries in higher and lower quintiles is broadly similar to the patterns for CPIA cluster D, in table 5.2.

Monitoring and Improving Public Finance and Administration

An effective bureaucracy is important for development. The bureaucracy formulates detailed policies that translate the goals of society and its political leaders into programs of action. It manages the implementation of these policies. And it reports on progress. Bureaucratic reform thus addresses both the upstream tasks of improving policy making and the operation of cross-cutting public financial management and administrative systems, and the downstream tasks of improving the performance of front-line service provision and regulatory agencies. This chapter focuses on options for monitoring and improving the upstream systems. Chapter 4 focuses on downstream systems.

Helping to build bureaucratic capability has long been a focus of development assistance. Before 2000, it was viewed as principally technocratic, with a gradual accumulation of lessons and advice on good practice. Even as these lessons crystallized, the profile of the work remained low because its focus on building country systems was at odds with the dominant approaches to providing aid and technical support through self-standing projects, hermetically sealed off from often dysfunctional public sectors. But with the new approach to aid placing increasing emphasis on mutual accountability, the profile of efforts to build bureaucratic capability has risen dramatically.

Better public policy making, financial management, and administration in developing countries would help resolve a seeming contradiction at the heart of the new aid architecture. On the one hand, the willingness of donors to forgive debt and to scale up aid is based on commitments by recipients to focus on poverty reduction in general, and the MDGs in particular. Thus, in December 1999, the PRS process was introduced as a new organizing framework for development support. One intention of the PRS process is that:

The development and implementation of poverty reduction strategies (PRS) [be] a precondition for access to debt relief and concessional financing from both [The World Bank and the International Monetary Fund.]. These strategies were expected to be poverty-focused, country-driven, results-oriented and comprehensive. They were also expected to serve as a framework for better coordination of development assistance among other development partners.[24]

On the other hand, the new architecture also aims to build on a hard-learned lesson of development experience—namely that externally imposed "conditionality" generally fails to achieve its intended results. The national budget—plus the public bureaucracy that prepares and implements the budget, and is accountable to its citizens—are the key vehicles for assuring real country ownership and leadership. As the PRS review highlights:

It is important for long-term visions to be adequately linked with medium-term strategies....In linking goals and targets to clear public actions, countries need to ascertain causal links...and make important choices with regard to prioritization and sequencing...Strengthening the link between the PRS and the budget process is essential to institutionalizing the PRS approach....[25]

Where bureaucratic capabilities and government commitment to poverty reduction are strong, budget support is the natural way to transfer resources to support a country's PRS objectives without undermining country ownership through excessive external oversight. But where governments focus less on poverty reduction and participation, are less constrained to be accountable to their citizens, and have less capacity, the combination of a PRS process and budget support does not offer a ready way of resolving the tension between country ownership and donor fiduciary obligations. While some countries are making progress in developing a long-term holistic vision for poverty reduction, and translating that vision into a coherent, medium-term, sequenced strategy, most have a long way to go. The PRS Review of 2005 reported survey data covering 59 countries, which concluded that only 7 had well-developed strategic programs (World Bank and IMF 2005, and World Bank Operational Policy and Country Services 2005). The majority of the remaining countries had activity under way, though not yet advanced to the point that long-term visions could serve as a reference point for policy makers.

This chapter considers some key aspects of country progress in moving from general assertions of development goals to the specific articulation, costing, and implementation of strategies for poverty reduction. The chapter first reports on progress in monitoring the quality of public expenditure management and highlights some patterns across countries revealed by monitoring. It also highlights emerging lessons about how to strengthen public expenditure management systems in different country settings. And it gives particular attention to a facet of reform especially relevant to governance: strengthening the transparency of budget management systems. The chapter then reports on efforts to monitor public administration, drawing on experience to offer practical guidance on how to improve administrative capability, both for developing countries on a path of improving governance, and for their development partners seeking to monitor progress. It concludes by highlighting options for scaling up aid.

Monitoring and Improving Public Financial Management

Public financial management is particularly relevant to the new aid architecture. It is key for getting results on the ground, and for assuring donors that aid resources are being used prudently. Setting the stage is a framework based on the 2005 report of the multi-agency PEFA partnership program (figure 2.1). That report synthesized the results of more than a half-dozen years of work by PEFA partners to develop a common platform for assessing the quality of public finance systems, including those in aid-recipient countries. The framework depicts four facets of the budget cycle:

FIGURE 2.1 Public Financial Management—a Performance Monitoring Framework

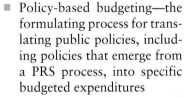

Source: PEFA Secretariat 2005, 4.

- Policy-based budgeting—the formulating process for translating public policies, including policies that emerge from a PRS process, into specific budgeted expenditures
- Arrangements for predictability, control, and stewardship in the use of public funds (for example, payroll and procurement systems)
- Systems of accounting and recordkeeping to provide information for proper management and accountability
- External audit and other mechanisms that ensure external scrutiny of the operations of the executive (for example, by parliament)

Comprehensiveness of budget coverage and transparency of fiscal and budget information cut across these four facets. The framework also identifies credibility—that the budget is realistic and implemented as intended—as a key intermediate outcome, a result of the operation of the whole cycle.

There are many ways of measuring the quality of a country's public financial management system. As box 2.1 highlights, the IMF has developed some useful tools.[26] This section focuses on two measures at two different levels—an overall measure of the quality of public expenditure management, and measures of specific expenditure management subsystems.

> ### BOX 2.1   Two IMF Tools to Support Fiscal Management and Transparency
>
> The Code of Good Practices on Fiscal Transparency was developed in response to concerns that a lack of comprehensive information on fiscal activity made it difficult to properly assess the objectives of fiscal policy. Greater fiscal transparency was also believed to be linked to improved governance and fiscal outcomes more generally. The code contains 37 good practices that are organized according to four main principles of fiscal transparency: clarity of roles and responsibilities; public availability of information; open budget preparation, execution, and reporting; and assurances of integrity. These practices, when observed, are critical not only for holding leaders accountable, but also for preventing any mishandling of finances during budget execution.
>
> The IMF regularly undertakes assessments of fiscal transparency called fiscal Reports on Observance of Standards and Codes (ROSCs) in its member countries. Participation in an ROSC is voluntary, and the authorities retain the right not to publish the final report, although most have agreed to do so.[27] As of the end of 2005, fiscal ROSCs have been completed for 80 countries, and 76 of these have been published. ROSC participation is distributed unevenly across regions, with most countries in Europe and the continental Western Hemisphere having completed ROSCs, while a much smaller share of countries in Africa, the Middle East, and Asia have agreed to participate. A number of countries, especially in Europe, have been working on improving fiscal transparency and have opted to undertake one or more ROSC updates to reflect this progress. In addition, a growing number of countries are undertaking full reassessments. Both reassessments and updates are published on the IMF Web site with the original ROSC.
>
> *Source:* International Monetary Fund, Fiscal Affairs Department, Fiscal Transparency Unit.

An Overall Assessment

The results of CPIA criterion 13 (see box 1.3)—abbreviated here as CPIA-budget—can be used to assess overall patterns in the quality of budget management systems across countries. Annex table 2.1 details the six-point quality rating used to score CPIA-budget. As a country improves its budget management system, its CPIA-budget score moves from weakest (1) to strongest (6). The scale is built from four dimensions of budget management, depicted by the (a)–(d) subcategories, which broadly correspond to the facets of the PEFA performance management framework in figure 7.1.[28] A CPIA-budget score at or above 4 is consistent with the "good enough governance" pattern described in chapter 1.

As of 2004, only 10 of 66 low-income aid-recipient countries had the "good enough" (though imperfect) budget system implied by a CPIA-budget score of 4 (figure 2.2). These higher-performing countries are Azerbaijan, Benin, Burkina Faso, India, Indonesia, Mali, Serbia and Montenegro, Sri Lanka, Tanzania, and Uganda. Almost half the countries scored at or below 3. Of the 10 better-performing countries, Azerbaijan, Mali, and Tanzania raised their CPIA-budget scores by at least one point between 2001 and 2004.

Disaggregated Public Financial Management Indicators

The HIPC debt-reduction initiative spurred a sustained effort to develop actionable indicators of budget quality. A first set of 16 indicators was developed jointly by the World Bank and the IMF, and applied in 2001 in 23 heavily indebted poor countries through a joint assessment with recipient-country governments, with a follow-up assessment in 2004.

Building directly on the HIPC tracking process, seven donors (the World Bank, the IMF, the European Commission, the UK Department for International Development [DFID], France, Norway, and Switzerland), plus the Strategic Partnership with Africa, embarked on a joint PEFA program to support "integrated and harmonized approaches to assessment and reform in the field of public expenditure, procurement, and financial accountability."[29] In 2005, PEFA issued its public financial management performance measurement framework, including 28 high-level monitoring indicators. Annex table 2.2 lists the high-level indicators and indicates how they are aligned with the earlier-generation HIPC tracking efforts (for which, as noted, measures are available for two periods in 23 countries). PEFA participants have committed to harmonizing their assessments of the quality of the public management systems of aid-recipient countries around the PEFA framework.

The HIPC tracking indicators score each question on an A–C scale, with detailed descriptions of how to score each question and an explicit benchmark of "good enough" performance for each question.[30] Table 2.1 aggregates the HIPC tracking results for 2004 for the 16 indicators into five categories aligned with the public financial management framework laid out in figure 2.1.

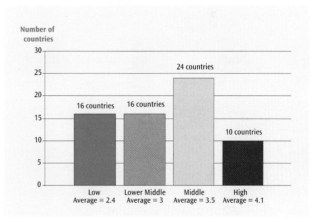

FIGURE 2.2 Low-Income Aid Recipient Countries by CPIA 13 (Quality of Budgetary and Financial Management) Score, 2004

Source: World Bank CPIA Database.

Control of procurement and payroll were not part of the 2001 HIPC tracking indicators. In practice, procurement and payroll—plus cash transfers—make up the overwhelming majority of public spending, so strong controls in these areas are vital for good financial management. Recent advances in monitoring the quality of procurement highlight some emerging lessons (box 2.2).

Consider first the cross-country patterns for policy-based budgeting. Done well, policy-based budgeting can sharpen the focus on longer-term priorities, enable phasing in shifts in priority expenditures over time, and potentially reconcile capital costs and their recurrent cost implications (if capital and recurrent budgets are integrated). The HIPC tracking indicator reported in the third column of table 2.1, labeled "policy-based budgeting," focuses on medium-term projections. A score of A signals that medium-term projections exist and are integrated into the budget formulation cycle; a score of B that they exist but are not integrated; a score of C that they exist for only a few sectors or not at all. In 2004, only 7 of the 25 countries tracked had integrated medium-term projections into their budget cycles, but 13 of the remaining countries made projections (but did not integrate them into the cycle).

Now consider the cross-country patterns for budget implementation in the fourth, fifth, and sixth columns in table 2.1:

TABLE 2.1   Quality of Budget Management Systems in 25 Heavily Indebted Poor Countries, 2004

CPIA-budget rating	Country	Policy-based budgeting (1 measure:[a] A–C ranking)	Budget comprehensiveness (4 measures:[b] # met)	Budget credibility (2 measures:[c] # met)	Budget execution (5 measures:[d] # met)	External budget scrutiny (2 measures:[e] # met)
Best-performing group (both CPIA and HIPC)	Mali	A	2	2	4	1
	Tanzania	A	2	2	4	1
	Burkina Faso	A	2	2	3	1
	Benin	A	2	1	4	0
	Uganda	A	1	0	3	2
Middle group 1	Guyana	B	3	2	2	2
	Chad	B	3	0	2	2
	Rwanda	A	1	1	2	2
	Senegal	B	2	2	3	0
	Ghana	B	1	1	3	1
	Honduras	B	2	1	2	1
Middle group 2	Cameroon	C	1	1	3	1
	Ethiopia	B	3	1	1	1
	Sierra Leone	C	2	1	2	1
	Bolivia	B	4	0	0	0
	Niger	B	2	0	2	0
	Guinea	B	2	0	2	1
	Malawi	B	2	0	2	0
	Madagascar	A	2	0	1	0
	Mozambique	B	1	2	0	1
	Zambia	B	0	0	1	2
Weaker-performing group	São Tomé and Principe	C	2	0	1	1
	Congo, Dem. Rep. of	C	2	0	0	0
	Gambia, The	B	2	0	0	0
	Guinea-Bissau	C	0	0	0	0

Source: IDA and IMF 2005. For details of the individual HIPC indicators, see
www1.worldbank.org/publicsector/pe/FinalHIPCAAPGuidance2003–04.pdf.
a. The measure is HIPC indicator 7.
b. The measures are HIPC indicators 1, 2, 4, 5.
c. The measures are HIPC indicators 3 and 8.
d. The measures are HIPC indicators 9–13.
e The measures are HIPC indicators 14–15.

■ The fourth column reports on measures of whether the budget is comprehensive, with no significant extra budgetary funds (including unfunded contingent liabilities), and with donor funds also reported. Only Bolivia, Chad, Ethiopia, and Guyana can be said to have comprehensive budgets in the sense that they met at least three of the four benchmarks. Seven countries met no more than one benchmark.

■ The fifth column reports on budget credibility, as measured by the closeness of actual expenditure out-turns (both aggregate and sectorally), compared with the original approved budget, and limits on the extent of arrears. Six countries have fully credible budgets (meet both indicators), but 12 countries met neither of the credibility benchmarks.

■ The sixth column reports on whether countries have a well-functioning expenditure execution system, including an internal audit mechanism, and other in-budget-year controls. Only 8 of the 25 countries met three or more of the five budget execution indicators tracked in the HIPC process, and 9 countries met only one or none.

Overall, seven countries (Benin, Burkina Faso, Guyana, Honduras, Mali, Senegal, and Tanzania) can be said to implement their budgets reasonably effectively, in the sense that they met the benchmarks for half or more of the criteria in each of columns 4–6. Another seven countries (Bolivia, Democratic Republic of Congo, The Gambia, Guinea-Bissau, Mozambique, Uganda, and Zambia) met fewer than half of the benchmarks in at least two of the three categories, and so appear to have significant weaknesses in budget implementation.

The seventh column of table 2.1 reports on the quality of budget reporting and external scrutiny. Adequate accounts are a precondition for effective scrutiny. As of 2004, 14 countries met one of the two benchmarks—closing annual accounts within two months of the end of the fiscal year. Formal oversight of the budget is the responsibility of parliament, based on independent audits of the accounts, and is measured by the second benchmark. But not one of the HIPC monitored countries submitted audited reports to its legislature within six months of the end of the fiscal year, and only seven countries submitted an audit within the benchmark of 12 months.

The results confirm that the quality of budget management systems of the 25 HIPC tracked countries remains uneven. Only Burkina Faso, Mali, and Tanzania score in the top half of possible (absolute) scores in all five categories. Ethiopia, Ghana, Guyana, Honduras, and Rwanda avoid the bottom rung in all categories. The remaining 17 countries have budget systems with at least one deep flaw.

This unevenness raises concern. The budget process is like a chain in the sense that it is only as strong as its weakest link. Even well-formulated budgets add modest value if there is little relation between the budget on paper and the way money is actually spent. And the impact of a well-prioritized and well-executed formal budget is undercut if much of the public spending is off budget.

Strengthening Public Financial Management

Why is performance on public financial management so uneven? In some countries poor performance may be a consequence of clientelism, extended civil conflict, and the evasion of formal rules and external scrutiny. Serious improvement is unlikely without changes in a country's political dynamics. This is more likely for some of the one-third or so of low-income aid-recipient countries that have consistently been stuck in the fourth and fifth quintiles of all governance performance measures, with no improvement over the past five years. In most cases, their capabilities have been undermined by conflict.

BOX 2.2   Recent Advances in Monitoring the Quality of Procurement

Despite its critical importance, until recently public procurement has often been treated as exclusively a technical exercise of marginal significance to governments and donors alike. Its emergence from the backroom of public sector operations has been accelerated by the emerging aid architecture, and its focus on country systems. Governments and advisers alike have increasingly recognized that the mechanisms by which the government purchases goods, works, and services, and the effectiveness of these practices, influence the financial well being of nations, the ability of citizens to access public services, and the competitiveness of domestic firms. Spending on procurement is at the core of government's discretionary spending; even minor improvements in efficiency can yield substantial cost savings.

Monitoring of public procurement systems has proliferated since 2002 through the creation of internationally accepted monitoring tools and innovative efforts by governments and nongovernment groups alike. The simplest form of monitoring procurement is the physical observation of procurement practices or outcomes. In Latvia and other countries, nongovernmental observers have become a feature of high-value procurements in order to ensure procedural regularity. Physical monitoring of procurement has also been enabled by countries through the creation of complaint response mechanisms that allow private parties to monitor the manner in which individual procurement operations are handled. A final mechanism that countries have developed to monitor procurement outcomes is the creation of asset registries that allow governments the ability to monitor how procured assets are used and maintained.

A second form of procurement monitoring is the publication of information on procurement opportunities and outcomes. The introduction of electronic procurement systems in many countries has tremendously increased the visibility of public contracting and allowed government and nongovernment bodies alike the opportunity to review the distribution of contract awards, as well as the price the government pays for its goods, works, and services. Countries as disparate as the Republic of Korea, Mexico, Romania, and Vietnam have made significant progress at greatly enhancing the transparency of public procurement through the use of informational technology. The increased transparency generated by the electronic procurement system in the Philippines has alone been credited with reducing costs by 10–15 percent.

(continued)

**BOX 2.2   Recent Advances in Monitoring the Quality
of Procurement (continued)**

A final form of procurement monitoring has involved assessing performance of public procurement systems utilizing defined performance indicators. Work on developing tools suitable for monitoring public procurement has been undertaken jointly by donors and partner countries over a two-year period. A procurement-specific indicator has been included in the PEFA Performance Indicators (see annex table 2.2, indicator 19), and an entire tool, the BIS, has been developed as part of the OECD-DAC Working Party on Improving Aid Effectiveness. The BIS has been adopted and utilized in more than 10 countries in the six months since it has been finalized.

As the example of the Phillipines' ambitious procurement reform program illustrates, these diverse monitoring mechanisms can be mutually reinforcing. Thus, in 2005 the government initiated work to measure public procurement performance in 10 of its largest agencies. The work complemented other procurement monitoring efforts going on in the country that included: the application of the OECD-DAC Baseline Indicator of Procurement Systems (BIS) tool; the observance of procurement proceedings by civil society representatives; and the publishing of information on the award of procurement contracts and other relevant statistics on the governments' e-bulletin Web site.

Source: World Bank.
Note: The BIS tool is available at www.oecd.org/dataoecd/12/14/34336126.pdf.

But many countries have shown the capacity for quite rapid improvement in their public financial management systems:

- The CPIA and HIPC tracking assessments reveal that many countries strengthened their budget systems in just three years—some substantially. Of the 66 IDA-recipient countries included here, 19 improved their CPIA-budget score between 2001 and 2004—7 of them by one or more points. A comparison between the 2001 and 2004 HIPC tracking assessments (figure 2.3) identifies six (Cameroon, Ghana, Mali, Niger, Senegal, and Tanzania) that improved their scores in a net of at least three categories.
- Even in a brief three-year time span, some countries made substantial improvements for each of the five budget subsystems. For budget execution, Senegal went from meeting none of the benchmarks in 2001 to meeting three in 2004, and Ghana from one to three. Cameroon improved its score on both "external scrutiny" benchmarks (though in 2004 it still took more than two months to close its annual accounts). Guinea's score on policy-based budgeting went from C to A. And Bolivia and Guyana increased by two the number of "budget comprehensiveness" benchmarks met.
- As the sustained improvements in Ghana, Mali, Senegal, and Tanzania suggest, countries with stronger starting capacity (measured, say, by having more benchmarks met in 2001) may be better able to achieve rapid gains in the short run

FIGURE 2.3 Net Change in HIPC Indicator Tracking Scores, 2001–04

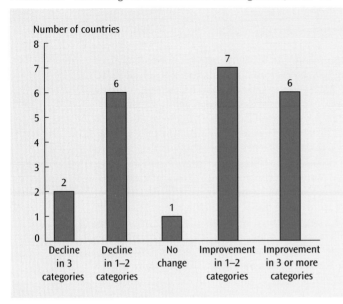

Number of countries

Source: IDA and IMF 2005, update on HIPC tracking.

than countries with weaker starting points.[31] But Niger—which improved its ranking in a net of five categories[32]—suggests that significant gains also are possible where the starting point is weak.

These patterns suggest that heightened attention to budget management and strong incentives for better performance can result in quite rapid gains. For countries determined to improve their public financial management systems, achieving a "good enough" standard within, say, a 5- to 10-year period may be feasible. How budget reform is designed and implemented will be key.

A first lesson for strengthening public financial management systems is that only a few countries—those with committed developmental leadership, plus a preexisting baseline of capacity—appear able to adopt and rapidly implement a comprehensive program of budget reform in most countries, the approach should be incremental. The reforms proposed for specific budget management subsystems have sometimes been very ambitious. Recent reviews by both the IMF and the World Bank have examined the experience with medium-term expenditure frameworks (MTEFs). The IMF review captures the shared conclusion, namely that "developing comprehensive medium-term expenditure frameworks can be effective when circumstances and capacities permit. Otherwise, it can be a great consumer of time and resources and might distract attention from the immediate needs for improving the annual budget and budget execution processes."

The IMF review also offers some useful guidance in noting that[33]

> ...the MTEF, as a feasible means of improving budgeting, requires the following: reliable macroeconomic projections, linked to fiscal targets in a stable economic environment; a satisfactory budget classification and accurate and timely accounting; technical capacity...and disciplined policy decision-making, [including] budgetary discipline...and political discipline for fiscal management. Before introducing an MTEF, one should raise a question: is the country ready for such an exercise in the sense of having adequate support for the above preconditions? When this support was not adequate in a number of African countries, the MTEF was introduced prematurely, and is turning out to be merely a paper exercise.

Efforts to install computerized financial management information systems also are often overambitious and invariably encounter significant delays. Reviews by both the World Bank and the IMF of efforts to install such systems in African countries concluded that large—and therefore more spectacular—projects are often preferred because they can be easily communicated as evidence of political action, but they are more volatile and subject to greater likelihood of failure than are smaller, more focused interventions.[34]

A useful guide to sequencing public financial management reform in low-capacity settings is suggested by DFID. The new "platform approach" for Cambodia involves a cumulative sequence of budget reforms that focuses each round on achieving specific budget functionalities, building on these functionalities in the subsequent round.[35] The sequence that emerges is almost the reverse of that often associated with PRS implementation (figure 2.4). Efforts to implement PRSs have focused on their costing and translation into medium-term budget frameworks and on strengthening countries' statistical capacities to monitor results.[36] By contrast, the Cambodian platform sequence focuses first on the basics: budget credibility, then predictability and control in budget execution. Only after these first two platforms are locked in will they move on to medium-term budget planning—and only once that is in place will they foster public management reforms to support a results culture throughout the public bureaucracy. Country leadership has been an important feature of Cambodia's public financial management program, ensuring that the design of reforms reflects domestic priorities, rather than those of donors.

A second emerging lesson for budget management is to complement the technocratic reforms with greater transparency. Although the PRS approach highlights inclusiveness, its implicit route to effectiveness tends to be technocratic: design a robust poverty-reducing budget, execute it effectively, monitor results, and recalibrate policy and budgeting on the basis of what is learned. The lesson emerging from experience is that, in developing countries with weaker capacity, this process may be better viewed as a long-run trajectory than as a feasible path to better results in the short to medium term. That explains interest in a more demand-side approach, complementing the technocratic route: along with participatory priority-setting in PRSs, foster transparency in budget management, and emphasize the potential of public information to improve the developmental discourse among citizens, their governments, and development partners.

Monitoring and Improving Administrative Quality

Attaining development results depends on much more than good financial management. For any organization, public or private, delivery depends on the quality not only of the financial side of its balance sheet, but also of its real side—the quality of its people, and how effectively they are deployed and led.

As the framework in chapter 1 highlighted, public administration comprises both downstream service provision and regulatory agencies (schools and ministries of education, customs agencies, roads authorities, and the like) and upstream cross-cutting control agencies within the bureaucracy (pay, human resource, and performance management control agencies, for example). Public administration reforms generally combine a focus on improving upstream systems—to have a broad impact across multiple systems—with targeted efforts to improve the performance of specific, high-priority agencies. This section focuses on upstream reforms; chapter 4 will consider agency and sector-specific approaches.

In the 1980s and early 1990s, a first generation of administrative reform focused principally on scaling back the bloated apparatus of government. In the late 1990s, attention shifted toward improving administrative capability. Some consensus has been generated on the characteristics of an effective public administration. As the CPIA subcategories used to score the "quality of public administration" (see annex table 2.3) suggest, the standard prescription typically includes the following:

■ Well-functioning mechanisms for policy coordination that ensure policy consistency across departmental boundaries and facilitate clear decisions on policy and spending priorities. To be effective, these coordinating mechanisms need to be at the apex of government, supported by top political leadership.

FIGURE 2.4   A Platform Approach to Budget Management Reforms in Cambodia

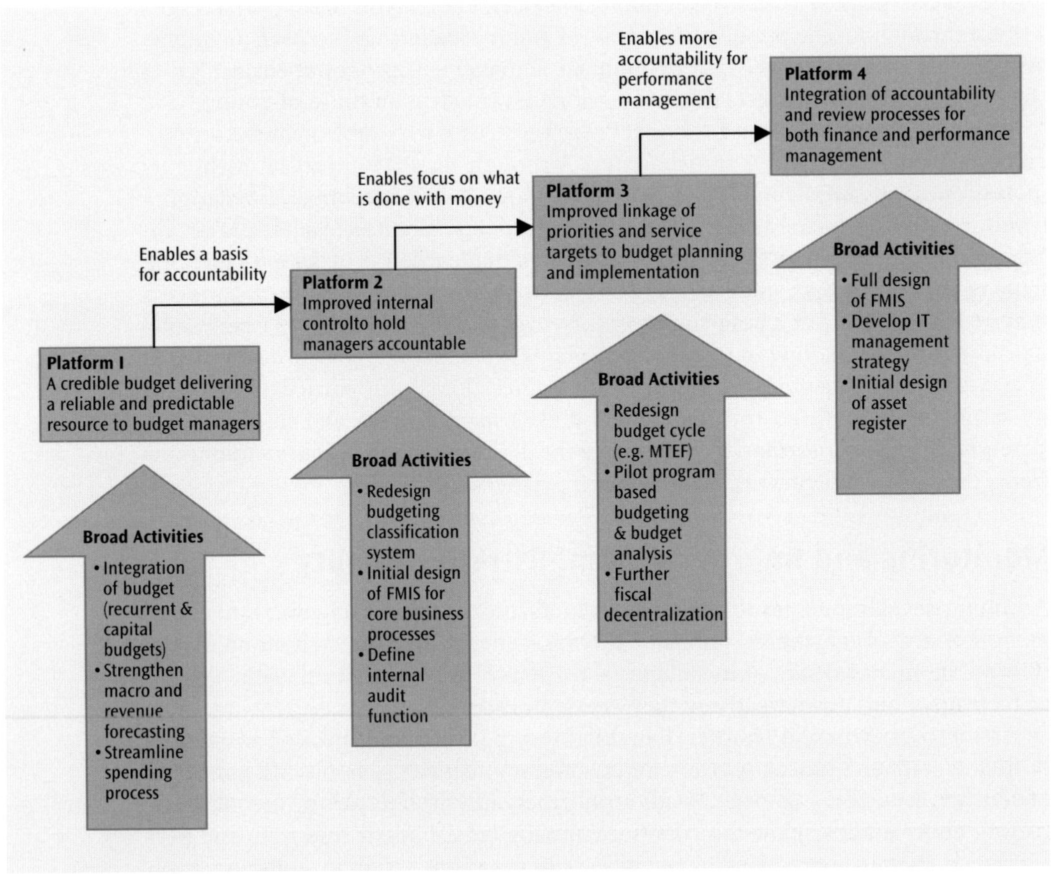

Source: DFID 2005.

- Well-designed administrative structures for individual line ministries and semiautonomous executive agencies, with little duplication of responsibility, and with clear lines of authority, plus streamlined business processes and a focus on results.
- Human resource management underpinned by the principle of meritocracy, including for recruitment, promotion, and major disciplinary actions. This includes insulation from undue political or personal interests, as well as practices that reward good performance (for example, through career advancement and financial rewards) and penalize poor performance.
- Pay and benefits adequate to attract and retain competent staff, including at senior and technical levels.
- Control over the aggregate wage bill sufficiently robust to ensure that the public sector wage bill is sustainable under overall fiscal constraints.

Monitoring Administrative Capability

As with CPIA-budget, the 1–6 scale of CPIA-admin describes the gradations for a country to move through as it works to improve the quality of its public administration.

The track record of efforts to close the gaps between the desired and actual quality of public administration is (to put it gently) uneven in both developed and developing countries. A landmark review of public administrative reform in 10 OECD countries—including such noted public management reformers as Australia, New Zealand, Sweden, the United States, and the United Kingdom—concluded:[37]

> Reform-watching in public management can be a sobering pastime. The gaps between rhetoric and actions…are frequently so wide as to provoke skepticism. The pace of underlying, embedded achievement tends to be much slower than the helter-skelter cascade of new announcements and initiatives. Incremental analysis and partisan mutual adjustment seem to have been very frequent features of public management reform, even if more-than-incremental changes were frequently hoped for.

The CPIA-admin scores provide a snapshot of administrative system performance and reform for the 66 IDA countries. The ability to measure is less well developed for administrative quality than for budget management. No disaggregated actionable measures paralleling the HIPC tracking and PEFA indicators are available—although an initiative to fill the gap is at an early stage of piloting (box 2.3).

Public administrative systems are weaker than their budget management counterparts (figure 2.5). Of the 66 IDA countries, only two score 4 or more on CPIA-admin (versus 10 on CPIA-budget), and only 17 score 3.5 (versus 24 on CPIA-budget). Trends in CPIA-admin suggest that, though change generally comes slowly, committed countries can achieve quite rapid improvement in their systems of public administration: Between 2001 and 2004, Armenia, Azerbaijan, Cameroon, Georgia, and Vietnam lifted their CPIA-admin scores by one or more points, more than any plausible margin of error.

A comparison of the results among low-income aid-recipient countries for CPIA-admin and CPIA-budget—and the relation between each and the corruption and-

BOX 2.3 Actionable Indicators on Public Administrative Quality

World Bank-supported operational work in Albania, FYR Macedonia, and Romania has yielded some actionable indicators to monitor the extent to which the immediate objectives of civil service management are being furthered. The table below identifies specific subobjectives for civil service management, and indicators to monitor each subobjective.

Civil service management actionable indicators

Objective	Indicator
Merit-based civil service (CS) management	
Competition in recruitment and selection	Percentage of CS vacancies filled through advertised, competitive procedures
Turnover unrelated to changes in political leadership	Quarterly CS turnover rates plotted against changes in political leadership
Effective performance evaluation practices	Percentage of CS staff for whom annual performance evaluations were completed
	Percentage of CS performance evaluations falling in each rating category
Attracting and retaining qualified staff	
Competitive remuneration	Average CS total remuneration as a percentage of average economic sector wages
	Ratios of average CS to private sector total remuneration by title
Vertical decompression	Ratio of average secretary general total remuneration to average junior officer total remuneration
Attracting qualified staff	Average number of qualified (long-listed) candidates per advertised CS opening
Continuously weeding out poor performing staff	Percentage of civil servants receiving the lowest performance rating in two successive years who have left the CS within the following year
Fiscally sustainable wage bill	
Budget-financed wage bill is fiscally sustainable	Actual budget-financed overall wage bill as a percentage of GDP

Albania was first to begin using these indicators (in early 2000). Three examples illustrate their impact on reform implementation. First, reformers documented a significant increase in requests from ministers for exemptions from the competitive recruitment procedures mandated by the CS law, and used the data to successfully make a case for imposing regulations that would make it more difficult to justify such exemptions. Second, a survey of public and private sector salaries was used to develop a new CS salary structure that would ensure consistency in the competitiveness of CS salaries across types of CS positions. Third, evidence on a rising incidence of qualified applicants per advertised CS position in Albania has helped to convince doubters about the efficacy of Albania's competitive recruitment and selection procedures.

Source: World Bank.

policy-quality outcomes—suggests some unevenness across governance subsystems.

The overall correlation between CPIA-budget and CPIA-admin is quite high at (0.73) (table 2.2). But the quality of budget management and of public administration can be very different from one country to another. Budget systems generally are stronger than their administrative counterparts. But Armenia, Bhutan, Malawi, and Madagascar depart from this overall pattern, with CPIA-admin scores above CPIA-budget scores. By contrast, Azerbaijan, Benin, Chad, Mali, Tanzania, and Uganda are exaggerated variants of the overall pattern, with CPIA-budget scores exceeding CPIA-admin scores by at least one point.

Patterns of change can be similarly uneven. Only Azerbaijan, Cameroon, and Haiti enjoyed rapid balanced improvements from 2001 to 2004 in both budget management and public administration—as measured by improvements of one or more points on each of the two CPIA measures. By contrast, Angola, Armenia, Burundi, Georgia, and Vietnam enjoyed disproportionate gains in public administration, while for Mali, Papua New Guinea, and Tanzania, the CPIA gains were disproportionate for budget management.

The correlation between budget systems and control over corruption is low, at 0.46. This result is not as surprising as it may appear at first—corruption is an outcome of the quality of national governance systems as a whole, not simply budget management (chapter 1), and can be unrelated to public expenditure management. Even so, the result highlights an acute dilemma for approaches to aid that give special prominence to improving budget systems to monitor the use of donor resources. The strong focus on strengthening budget management may help in underpinning good resource allocation and related policies, but not prove a panacea in the fight against corruption. Greater clarity is needed in the global dialogue on governance, corruption, and development impact as to what is achievable, and how it can realistically be achieved.

Strengthening Administrative Capability

Building effective public administrative systems in developing countries is difficult. A 1999 review of 102 World Bank operations to support civil service reform between 1987 and 1997 found that only 33 percent of closed civil service reform interventions and 38 percent of ongoing efforts achieved satisfactory outcomes.[38] Useful lessons are emerging as to both the reasons for the disappointing track record of efforts to improve administrative systems, and constructive options for proceeding.[49]

Much of the administrative reform agenda aims to improve processes, and process reforms tend to be soft, with progress difficult to observe or measure. Even when these reforms work, their impact is evident only over the long term. From the start, though, they threaten the authority of established interests throughout the bureaucracy. Resistance to reform within the bureaucracy—either overt, or through halfhearted implementation—is therefore likely to be endemic.

Then there is the political logic of reform. Political leaders need to balance a technocratic view of good reform practice with the political imperatives of building and sustaining alliances with powerful patrons, avoiding conflict with powerful social groups, and maintaining electoral support. Such a calculus is not favorable for seri-

FIGURE 2.5 Low-Income Aid-Recipient Countries by CPIA 15 (Quality of Public Administration) Score, 2004.

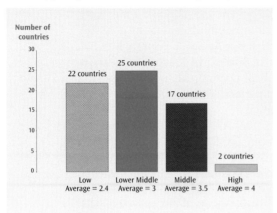

Source: World Bank CPIA Database.

ous administrative reform: the upfront political costs are substantial, and the time horizon is long before benefits are evident in the form of improved public performance. It is, however, much more favorable for more cynical politicians with a short time horizon to promise bold reforms to clean up government and get government working, in full knowledge that the seriousness—or otherwise—of the reform effort will be invisible to the average citizen.

The implication for reform design is straightforward. Achieve a good fit, aligning the administrative reform agenda in a realistic way to a country's political realities on the ground. Then proceed with rapid, comprehensive administrative reform only in those rare cases where there is a strong enough baseline of capacity for sustained administrative reform and political leadership with the commitment, mandate, and time horizon needed to see the effort through. Without such capacity and leadership, the approaches have to be more explicitly incremental and cumulative in their consequences.

Three successful good-fit administrative reformers—Albania, Latvia, and Tanzania—are positioned at different starting points on the capacity-leadership spectrum, so their reform programs have varied in the ambition of what they have attempted.

Latvia, of the three, has the most propitious environment for comprehensive administrative reform, with strong human capacity in its public sector. Since the mid-1990s, it has demonstrated sound economic management. And the incentive of accession to the European Union provided powerful continuing momentum for reform.

As table 2.3 details, between 2000 and 2003, the country promulgated an ambitious, and generally well-regarded, agenda of administrative reform including: a new civil service law that guaranteed meritocratic recruitment and introduced performance appraisal; a new control framework for the large number of semiautonomous state agencies; and a new framework for coordinating policy-making and administrative reform from the Prime Minister's Office. It also made ongoing efforts to reform the public sector salary structure.

Perhaps most striking about the Latvian experience is not so much the ambition of what was attempted, but how challenging implementation is proving to be. The passage of reformist legislation proceeded straightforwardly. But in the face of entrenched political interests, patronage persists in civil service recruitment (even though the rules of the game have changed profoundly). Realigning the structures of ministries and state agencies and implementing the newly legislated control framework have proceeded slowly—still only partly completed, five years after passage of the key legislation. Political inertia and difficult technical challenges have repeatedly disrupted efforts to change the public salary structure. The point is not that Latvia should have taken a less bold approach, or that it has been a laggardly

TABLE 2.2   Bureaucratic Capability and Governance Outcomes—Some Correlations

	CPIA-budget	CPIA-admin
CPIA-admin	0.73	1.00
CPIA-policies	0.80	0.78
KK corruption	0.46	0.69

Source: Author.

implementer—it is to underscore that, even in the best of circumstances, administrative reform is a long-term process, with progress achieved in fits and starts.

Tanzania's evident strengths as it embarked on administrative reform were its political institutions and culture—formal state institutions with broad social legitimacy, a dominant political party with a culture of consensual decision making, and a unifying identity as a nation, painstakingly nurtured over three decades. Its challenges: the absence of a consensus on the way forward in the wake of an economically disastrous experience with African socialism, and severely weakened public capacity to initiate and implement reforms.

The momentum of administrative reform built incrementally, sustaining a consensus as the program unfolded. An eight-year (1991–99) civil service program first brought employment and the wage bill under control, and then clarified the appropriate roles—and rightsizing—across a wide range of government ministries, departments, and agencies. Building on this success, Tanzania embarked in 2000 on an ambitious, 11-year program to transform the public sector into a service with capacity, systems, and culture to serve clients and continually improve services.

The approach to reform has been innovative, incremental, and set in a context of ambitious medium- to long-term goals:

■ A Performance Improvement Model is being rolled out to more than two dozen ministries and agencies. Each agency is given support to clarify its role and mission, develop a strategic plan (including well-defined results, and a well-publicized service delivery charter), and identify its capacity development needs. A Performance Improvement Fund helps implement the capacity development plans of agencies that have traversed the process.

■ With a new medium-term pay policy to enhance the attractiveness of public sector employment, especially at higher levels, a selective accelerated salary enhancement scheme will reward ministries and agencies that effectively implement the Performance Improvement Model by accelerating their transition to the new pay schedule. Selective implementation, while proving politically contentious, continues.

Fifteen years after the outset of its program, administrative reform continues to be a work in progress in Tanzania. But momentum has been sustained throughout—to the point that in 2006 Tanzania is regarded as the most successful low-income administrative reformer in Sub-Saharan Africa.

Albania offered the least propitious environment for administrative reform. To be sure, it enjoyed some advantages similar to Latvia's—a rapidly expanding economy, a more open society, proximity to Western Europe, and some prospect of eventual accession to the European Union. But in the wake of communism, skepticism about the value of state authority and collective action was pervasive. And politics was fiercely competitive, factionalized, and patronage based. There was no appetite or capacity for far-reaching administrative reform. Even so, Albania's administrative system made important gains between 1998 and 2005.

The gains came through the skillful exploitation, by both domestic reformers and their international champions, of a window of opportunity that opened between 1998 and 2002: the appointment (by the political leaders of an electorally victorious political party) of a reformist prime minister willing to champion an administrative reform agenda. Backstopped by strong conditionality from the World Bank, the agenda was carefully calibrated to be feasible in a setting with limited commitment to reform. Albania's administrative reform focused narrowly on introducing meritocracy, plus market-competitive pay, for the country's top 1,300 civil servants. Targeting only this top tier is not enough for systemwide improvements, but it can yield important gains in the quality of policy making and, more broadly, in the management of public resources. It can also establish a precedent of new ways of doing business, with the scope of application broadening over time. (The creation in Albania of an independent appeals body, the Civil Service Commission, to which aggrieved civil servants could appeal what they considered to be unjustified personnel management decisions, is an example of an important new precedent.)

In 2002, the reformist prime minister was replaced, and momentum shifted away from reform and toward Albanian politics as usual. Yet the reforms, which had been widely publicized and enjoyed both the support of donors and broad approval among Albania's citizens, had crowded in a powerful constituency for their continuation—the senior civil servants. The arrangements for a meritocracy have largely been sustained. Indeed, in 2005, parliament intervened directly to reject legislation that would have reduced the ability of the Department of Public Administration to enforce the promeritocracy 1999 civil service law.

A review of the CPIA and other governance indicators suggests that Albania's unpropitious environment for administrative reform is not uncommon. What makes Albania instructive for other similarly challenged countries is its embrace of a narrow agenda. Such an approach can build a platform for stronger public capability. But if the progress and impact of upstream reforms are not readily visible, they may be too narrow to turn around the broad performance of government—and they remain vulnerable to reversal.

What All This Means for Scaling Up Aid

As noted in the introduction to this chapter, well-functioning and transparent budget, administrative, and procurement systems—and a political process responsive to the country's citizenry—facilitate scaling up assistance, including that through budget support.

TABLE 2.3   Public Administrative Reform in Three Countries

Reform area (as per CPIA-admin)	Latvia	Tanzania	Albania
Top-level policy and reform coordination	2002: Strengthen coordination role of State Chancellery in Prime Minister's Office	1991: Empower Civil Service Department in Office of the President to lead public service reform	1998–2002: Delegated by reformist prime minister to Department of Public Administration
Organizational structures and processes	*2001 Law on Agencies* provides new control framework for semi-autonomous state agencies (implementation ongoing) 1999 program initiated to undertake functional reviews in all 12 ministries (6 completed by end of 2003)	*Civil Service Reform Program:* 1991–9 restructuring of 21 ministries and agencies. *Public Service Reform Program 2000–2011:* (i) creation and implementation of new executive agency framework (19 agencies created); (ii) rollout of Performance Improvement Model across all ministries and agencies; (iii) identification and financing of requisite capacity development	Sector-specific initiatives, including functional reviews of the Council of Ministers, and Ministries of Finance and Justice
Meritocratic human resource management	*2000 Civil Service Law* guarantees meritocratic recruitment, and introduces performance appraisal; implementation continuing	*PSRP:* introduction of performance appraisal system, linked to department-level strategic plans and objectives	*1999 Law on the Status of the Civil Servant* mandated transparent, competitive recruitment procedures for senior civil servants, formal performance appraisals, and created an independent appeals body
Public sector pay and employment	Concept for new salary structure adopted in 2000; scheme adopted in 2002; revised in 2003	*CSRP:* decompression of top-level pay (from 9:1 to 21:1 ratio). PSRP: adoption of new medium-term pay policy and SASE scheme	2002 core civil service cadre salaries increased to levels competitive with private sector comparators

Source: World Bank staff.

For most low-income aid recipients, this easy resolution is not straightforward. Interpreting "good enough governance" expansively, perhaps about 20 low-income aid recipients currently have budget management and administrative systems reasonably capable of targeting spending on poverty reduction priorities, and of executing and monitoring spending in a comprehensive, credible, and transparent way. With a few exceptions, World Bank budget support via Poverty Reduction Support

Credits has been targeted to these institutionally stronger countries, in the upper quintiles of the CPIA.[40]

What might be the "mutual accountability" basis for scaling up aid in the remaining countries? Three possibilities are worthy of note:

First, even where current systems fall short, budget support might be scaled up for countries based on a clearly improving trend in the quality of their budget and administrative management systems. This is not simply because the additional resource transfers can be poverty reducing: a shift from project aid to budget support can also be seen as an investment in strengthening country systems.[41] As the principles of the Paris Declaration on Aid Effectiveness underscore, heavily fragmented project aid complicates and disrupts national systems, whereas budget support, combined with technical assistance, can facilitate the improvement of these systems, particularly if scaling up depends on continuing system improvements. Tanzania illustrates this potential: it has shown rapid improvement in budget management systems since 2001, and has been a beneficiary of progressively scaled-up budget support over the period. The other examples highlighted in this chapter suggest that, for countries determined to improve their administrative budget systems, achieving a "good enough" standard within, say, 5 to 10 years may be feasible. Budget support might be initiated quite early in the cycle of improvement, and scaled up as long as the carefully monitored improvement continues to be evident.

Second, priority could be given to reforms that foster transparency—in budget management and more broadly. Transparency relies on public information as a source of pressure for better public sector performance in a less technocratic way than is implied by top-down reforms of bureaucratic capability. To be sure, the route from transparency to performance is circuitous, and the timing of impact is unpredictable. So far, no study definitively pinpoints the relationship between transparency and performance. But many examples, including some in this report, highlight the potential—from the tracking of education expenditures in Uganda, to service delivery report cards in Bangalore and Brazil, to the impact of media prevalence across India's states. Even with continuing weakness in bureaucratic capability, a case could thus be made for scaling up aid (including some component of budget support) to countries that clearly commit themselves to facilitating transparency in how public resources—and state power more broadly—are used.

The third possibility for countries is to target scaled-up aid more directly toward poverty-reducing services, which can be done in several ways. A key distinction here is between countries where bureaucratic capability may be on the upturn but is only at an early stage of improvement, and those where there is little sign of political commitment to improve governance and capacity. In the former group, sectorwide approaches that focus on improving governance and service provision in part of the overall system are attractive; sectoral approaches are discussed in chapter 4. In the latter group, the focus might be on infrastructure and other service delivery investment projects—complete with project implementation units and related mechanisms that operate apart from country systems. Box 4.2 will detail some well-founded objections to these approaches. But where there is little political commitment to improve country systems and little sign that governments would have targeted pro-poor spending, these objections have less relevance.

ANNEX TABLE 2.1 CPIA—Quality of Budget and Financial Management

(1= Weakest; 6 = Strongest)

1 a. If there is a budget, it is not a meaningful instrument, nor an indicator of policies or tool for allocation of public resources. More than 50 percent of public resources from all sources do not flow through the budget.

b. There is practically no monitoring and reporting of public expenditures. There is no reconciliation of cash accounts with fiscal accounts. No regular, in-year fiscal reports are produced.

c. Public accounts are seldom prepared, or are more than five years out of date. The use of public resources is not on the public agenda.

d. There is no information on revenues and expenditures at different levels of government. If at all, revenues and expenditures are assigned to different levels of government only on an ad hoc basis.

2 a. The budget is formulated without consultation with spending ministries. There is no discernible link with government policies or priorities, including poverty reduction. Significant fiscal operations (e.g., extrabudgetary expenditures, donor-funded projects, and contingent liabilities of 25–50 percent of total spending by value) are excluded from the budget.

b. There is no adequate system of budget reporting and monitoring, and no consistent classification system. There are significant payments arrears, and actual expenditures often deviate significantly from the amounts budgeted (e.g., by more than 30 percent overall or on many broad budget categories).

c. There are significant delays (more than three years) in the preparation of the public accounts. The accounts are not (professionally) audited or submitted to the legislature in a timely way, and no actions are taken on budget reports and audit findings.

d. There is no clear assignment of revenues and expenditures between different levels of government, and there is a significant mismatch of revenues and expenditures at each level.

3 a. Policies or priorities that may focus on poverty reduction are explicit, but are not linked to the budget. There is no forward looking in the budget. The budget is formulated in consultation with spending ministries. A significant amount of funds controlled by the executive is outside the budget (e.g., 10–25 percent), a number of donor activities bypass the budget, and there is no analysis of contingent liabilities.

b. The budget classification system does not provide an adequate picture of general government activities, and budget monitoring and control systems are inadequate. Payment arrears are a problem, and expenditures deviate from the amounts budgeted by more than 20 percent overall, or on many broad budget categories.

c. There are significant delays (more than two years) in the preparation of public accounts. Accounts are not audited in a timely and adequate way, and few if any actions are taken on budget reports and audit findings.

d. The assignment of revenues and expenditures between different levels of government is vague and there is a mismatch of revenues and expenditures.

4 a. Policies and priorities that focus on poverty reduction are broadly reflected in the budget. Some elements of forward budget planning are in place. The budget is prepared in consultation with spending ministries.

b. The budget classification system is comprehensive, but different from international standards. There are no significant extrabudgetary funds and nearly all donor funds are reported in the budget, but there is little analysis of contingent liabilities. Budget monitoring and control systems exist, but there are some deficiencies. Actual expenditures deviate from the amounts budgeted by more than 10 percent on many broad budget categories.

c. There are delays (more than one year) in preparation of the public accounts. The accounts are audited in a timely and professional manner, but few meaningful actions are taken on budget reports or audit findings.

d. The assignment of revenues and expenditures between different levels of government is clear, but there is still some mismatch of revenues and expenditures.

(continued)

ANNEX TABLE 2.1   CPIA—Quality of Budget and Financial Management (continued)

5 a. Policies and priorities focus on poverty reduction and are linked to the budget. The budget is formulated through systematic consultations with spending ministries and the legislature.

b. The budget classification system is comprehensive. Budget monitoring occurs throughout the year based on well-functioning management information systems. The budget is implemented as planned, and actual expenditures deviate only slightly from planned levels (e.g., by less than 10 percent on most broad categories).

c. The public accounts are prepared on a timely basis. The accounts are audited and submitted to the legislature in a timely way, and appropriate action is taken on budget reports and audit findings.

d. The assignment of revenues between different levels of government is clear and there is a good match of revenues and expenditures at each level of government.

6. Criteria for "5" on all four subratings are fully met. There are no warning signs of possible deterioration, and there is widespread expectation of continued strong or improving performance.

Source: http://siteresources.worldbank.org/IDA/Resources/CPIA2005Questionnaire.pdf.

ANNEX TABLE 2.2   The PEFA PFM Performance Indicator Set

		Included in HIPC Tracking?
	A. PFM-OUT-TURNS: Credibility of the Budget	
PI-1	Aggregate expenditure out-turn compared to original approved budget	Yes (H3)
PI-2	Composition of expenditure out-turn compared to original approved budget	Yes (H3)
PI-3	Aggregate revenue out-turn compared to original approved budget	
PI-4	Stock and monitoring of expenditure payment arrears	Yes (H8)
	B. KEY CROSS-CUTTING ISSUES: Comprehensiveness & Transparency	
PI-5	Classification of the budget	Yes (H5)
PI-6	Comprehensiveness of information included in budget documentation	Yes (H1)
PI-7	Extent of unreported government operations	Yes (H2; 4)
PI-8	Transparency of intergovernmental fiscal relations	
PI-9	Oversight of aggregate fiscal risk from other public sector entities	
PI-10	Public access to key fiscal information	
	C. BUDGET CYCLE	
	C(i) Policy-Based Budgeting	
PI-11	Orderliness and participation in the annual budget process	
PI-12	Multiyear perspective in fiscal planning, expenditure policy, and budgeting	Yes (H7)
	C(ii) Predictability and Control in Budget Execution	
PI-13	Transparency of taxpayer obligations and liabilities	
PI-14	Effectiveness of measures for taxpayer registration and tax assessment	
PI-15	Effectiveness in collection of tax payments	
PI-16	Predictability in the availability of funds for commitment of expenditures	
PI-17	Recording and management of cash balances, debt, and guarantees	
PI-18	Effectiveness of payroll controls	Yes (H9)
PI-19	Competition, value for money, and controls in procurement	
PI-20	Effectiveness of internal controls for nonsalary expenditure	Yes (H9)
PI-21	Effectiveness of internal audit	Yes (H9)
	C(iii) Accounting, Recording and Reporting	
PI-22	Timeliness and regularity of accounts reconciliation	Yes (H11)
PI-23	Availability of information on resources received by service delivery units	Yes (H10)
PI-24	Quality and timeliness of in-year budget reports	Yes (H12;13)
PI-25	Quality and timeliness of annual financial statements	Yes (H14)
	C(iv) External Scrutiny and Audit	
PI-26	Scope, nature, and followup of external audit	Yes (H15)
PI-27	Legislative scrutiny of the annual budget	
PI-28	Legislative scrutiny of external audit reports	

Source: PEFA June 2005, 9.

ANNEX TABLE 2.3   CPIA—Quality of Public Administration

1= weakest; 6= strongest

1 a. Mechanisms for coordination are nonexistent or ineffectual, creating bureaucratic conflict and uncertain or conflicting policies.

b. Administrative structures are highly fragmented, with vague and overlapping responsibilities. Business processes are extremely complex and convoluted, with multiple decision layers, and many signatures required to move decisions forward.

c. There are no workable rules on hiring and promotion, which are based on bribes, personal ties, or ethnic affiliation rather than merit. Most public employees, even at lower levels, lose their positions on changes in government. Bribe seeking is endemic.

d. Level of public employment has little relation to provision of public services: either employment is too low or too few employees show up for work to provide essential services, or the wage bill consumes all current spending, leaving no funds available for essential supplies, such as drugs or textbooks. Pay and benefit levels, particularly at upper levels, are a small fraction of comparable private sector levels, and bribe payments represent a large share of income for many public officials.

2 a. Mechanisms for coordination are weak.

b. Administrative structures are fragmented, with frequently overlapping responsibilities. Business processes are complex, involving multiple decision layers, regularly causing unnecessary delays.

c. Hiring and promotion based on personal ties or time in service rather than merit. Most public employees serve at the pleasure of the current government, and bribe seeking is accepted behavior.

d. Public employment as a share of total employment is clearly excessive. The wage bill represents an inordinate share of recurrent spending, with adverse impacts on the quality of public service delivery. Pay and benefit levels, particularly at upper levels, are far below comparable private sector levels, but benefits (housing, car, utilities, servants) for senior civil servants may be high, and there are other complex and opaque forms of compensation. "Ghost" employees are on the payroll.

3 a. Administrative structures are fragmented, and coordination mechanisms are generally inadequate to overcome parochial bureaucratic interests.

b. Business processes can be overly complex, often causing unnecessary delays.

c. Hiring and promotion are formally merit based, but there is extensive patronage in practice in several parts of government. Bribe seeking is accepted behavior in some agencies but not throughout government.

d. Public employment as a share of total employment is higher than needed and unsustainable if adequate wages were paid. The wage bill represents an excessively large proportion of total government expenditure. Some sectors are overstaffed (particularly health and education). Pay and benefit levels are generally inadequate and there are major difficulties in attracting and retaining staff in key technical areas.

4 a. Mechanisms for policy coordination generally function effectively.

b. Administrative structures are generally well designed, although gaps or areas of overlap may exist. Initial efforts have been made to redesign business processes in selected areas.

c. Hiring and promotion are merit based, but emphasize seniority unduly. Corruption may occur, but is not general practice in any public agency.

d. Public employment as a share of total employment is somewhat higher than needed and the wage bill represents a large proportion of government spending. Pay and benefit levels are low but not unattractive when benefits and job security are factored in. Some sectors are overstaffed (particularly health and education) and there are some difficulties in attracting and retaining staff in key technical areas.

(continued)

ANNEX TABLE 2.3: CPIA—Quality of Public Administration (continued)

5 a. Effective coordination mechanisms ensure a high degree of policy consistency across departmental boundaries.

b. Organizational structures are along functional lines, with very little duplication. Business processes are regularly reviewed to ensure efficiency of decision making and implementation.

c. Hiring and promotion are based on merit and performance, and ethical standards prevail.

d. The wage bill is sustainable and does not crowd out spending required for public services. Pay and benefit levels do not deter talented people from entering the public sector. There is flexibility (that is not abused) in paying more attractive wages in hard-to-fill positions (e.g., rural teachers, technical specialists).

6 Criteria for "5" on all four subratings are fully met. There are no warning signs of possible deterioration, and there is widespread expectation of continued strong, or improving, performance.

Notes

24. The World Bank and the International Monetary Fund 2005, 1, 10.

25. Ibid, 12, 15, 19.

26. For details of, and results from, the Code of Fiscal Transparency, see http://www.imf.org/external/np/fad/trans/index.htm.

27. All the published reports are available on the IMF ROSC Web site at http://www.imf.org/external/np/rosc/rosc.asp?sort=topic\#FiscalTransparency.

28. The correspondence between CPIA-budget and the PEFA PFM framework in figure 7.1 is as follows: (a) corresponds to policy-based budgeting, the formulating process; (b) corresponds to a combination of the comprehensiveness of budget coverage, credibility that the budget is realistic and implemented as intended, plus the budget execution arrangements for the exercise of predictability, control, and stewardship in the use of public funds; (c) corresponds to the systems of accounting and recordkeeping to provide the information needed for proper management, plus auditing mechanisms that ensure external scrutiny. Intergovernmental finance—the focus of (d)—is not directly incorporated in the PEFA framework.

29. See the PEFA Web site at http://www.pefa.org/index2.htm.

30. For some questions the benchmark was set at the score of B and for others at A. Further details, including the descriptions of how to score each question, are available at http://www.pefa.org/about_test.htm.

31. Dorotinsky, Kisunko, and Pradhan 2005.

32. Niger's ranking improved in eight categories and declined in three. Five of the improvements were sufficient to achieve the benchmark (but all three declines were from benchmark level to below).

33. IMF 2005.

34. IMF 2005; Heidenhof and others 2002.

35. DFID 2005.

36. See, for example, the Africa Action Plan recently issued by the World Bank.

37. Pollitt and Bouckaert 2000, 184, 188–89.

38. World Bank, Operations Evaluation Department (1999: ii–iii). The OED review highlighted four specific weaknesses in Bank-supported interventions: the poor quality of information on civil service reform performance needed for monitoring and evaluation; the

limited role afforded to strategic management and cultural change; the absence of checks and balances on arbitrary action; and a failure to appreciate key contextual contexts.

39. See the articles by Mike Stevens and StefanieTeggemann; Kithinji Kiragu, Rwekaza Mukandala, and Denyse Morin; Poul Engberg-Pedersen and Brian Levy in Levy and Kpundeh (2004).

40. See Gelb and Eifert (2005).

41. See Gelb and Eifert (2005) for this argument.

3

Monitoring and Improving National Checks-and-Balances Institutions

S trong checks-and-balances institutions are key to a well-functioning national governance system. Some of these checks and balances are global (including global financial and other markets).[42] The focus here is on national checks-and-balances institutions. Developmental leadership or a dynamic political movement can sometimes substitute for weak checks and balances, at least for a period. But over the longer run, well-functioning checks-and-balances institutions are key for *sustainability*. They help keep the executive arm of government focused on the public purpose. They are vital for fighting corruption; for ensuring that state actors at all levels use public resources efficiently and effectively; and for helping to ensure that citizens perceive state institutions to be legitimate.

Figure 3.1 disaggregates checks and balances into a constellation, arranged in terms of their "distance" from the executive authority they oversee. The relationship of these institutions with one another is only loosely hierarchical. Depending on a country's constitution, the judiciary may or may not be a constraint on legislative authority. Citizens may ultimately elect governments, but on a day-to-day basis their role is more participatory than hierarchical. We can distinguish three broad groups:

- An "inner constellation" of direct oversight—subnational governments, autonomous oversight agencies, and the legislature
- A "middle constellation" of impartial dispute resolution—in particular the justice system
- An "outer constellation" of civic voice—the rules (for example on freedom of information) and actors (such as the media) that ensure the open operation of

FIGURE 3.1 A "Constellation" of Checks-and-Balances Institutions

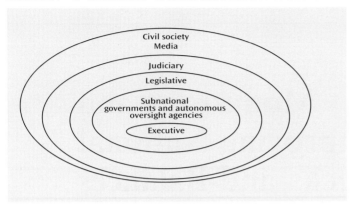

Source: Author.

civil society—and the transparent flow of information and data that enables citizens to play an informed role in public discourse. (Though not an explicit focus in this GMR, the discipline provided by competitive markets is an important buttress of this outer constellation.)

The next three sections will consider each of these in turn, discussing approaches to monitoring the quality of the relevant checks-and-balances institutions and highlighting how some can be strengthened. The final section considers the sequencing of checks-and-balances reforms in the context of the larger development effort. Four key themes emerge:

- Measurement of checks-and-balances institutions confronts a similar tension between broad and specific indicators, as does measurement in other governance areas. The most useful indicators are "actionable," capable of drilling down to identify strengths and weaknesses at increasing levels of disaggregation. A promising initiative is under way to develop actionable checks-and-balances indicators.
- The quality of checks and balances tends to be uneven, within as well as across countries. Rule of law can be weak even if restraints on the executive are strong. Citizens may enjoy open civic voice, but other restraints on the executive may be modest. Bureaucratic quality (as monitored in chapter 2) and the quality of checks and balances also are unevenly distributed, which creates some dilemmas for a country's development partners.
- Knowledge of how to strengthen checks-and-balances institutions remains rudimentary, but one emerging lesson is that formal arrangements are embedded within a larger political economy. Dysfunctional institutions are not generally amenable to technocratic quick fixes.
- Transparency appears to hold special promise as a relatively low-cost and low-key way of initiating a cumulative process of improvement in public debate, public advocacy, and government accountability to civil society. This highlights the role of information and statistical data, and the rules that govern open access to government information.

The Inner Constellation—Direct Oversight

Direct oversight institutions in the first two rings of figure 3.1 include elected subnational authorities, ombudsmen, supreme audit institutions (with independent authority to review national accounts, monitor the probity with which public resources are used, and report on their findings to parliament), anticorruption agencies (with independent authority to investigate and sometimes also to prosecute accusations of corruption), and the national legislature, to which the executive generally is directly accountable. This section considers options for monitoring the quality of direct oversight institutions, and highlights some challenges of improving the performance of two of these—legislatures and subnational authorities.

Monitoring Direct Oversight

One of the most widely used aggregate indicators is the "executive constraint" measure of the POLITY data set.[43] This measure refers to:

> ...the extent of institutionalized constraints on the decision-making powers of the executive. Such limitations may be imposed by any "accountability group." In Western democracies these are usually legislatures. Other kinds of accountability groups are the ruling party in a one-party state; councils of nobles or powerful advisors in monarchies, the military in coup prone poli ties; and in many states a strong, independent judiciary.[44]

POLITY IV scores on a seven-point scale. Box 3.1 details the criteria for ratings of 1, 5 and 7.[45] Table 3.1 groups the POLITY IV results for 60 low-income countries into four categories: low (score of 1 or 2); medium (score of 3 or 4); medium-high (score of 5 or 6); and high (score of 7). Data are for 2004, the most recent year available. Most OECD and many middle-income countries score in the high and medium-high categories, but many countries that confront difficult governance issues also score medium-high on the indicator. The reason for the latter is that a country's political and bureaucratic leadership can find itself constrained either as part of a well-functioning overall institutional environment, or as part of an overall syndrome of state weakness. The last section of the chapter will consider this issue further.

More disaggregated measures of the quality of direct oversight are provided by the "Global Integrity Index" (GII) prepared by the independent nongovernmental organization, Global Integrity. As box 3.2 describes, the GII is an example of "good practice" methodology for governance indicators. As explained earlier, as with all governance indicators, the estimates have some margin of error. But because each measure is specifically defined, it provides "actionable" information for governance reform.

Table 3.2 reports the scores for four narrowly focused GII subindicators that most directly monitor the quality of direct oversight agencies.[46] In most OECD and some middle-income countries, restraints on the executive are rated as high; Zimbabwe stands out among the low-income countries considered as having few effective executive constraints.

Strengthening Legislative Oversight

Approximately 90 percent of the world's nearly 200 sovereign countries have national legislatures or parliaments. Over the past 15 years, more than a quarter have revised their constitutions to include an expanded role for their legislatures.

BOX 3.1 The POLITY IV Executive Constraints' Criteria

Rating of 1—Unlimited authority.
There are no regular limitations on the executive's actions.

Examples of evidence:
i.   Constitutional restrictions on executive action are ignored.
ii. Constitution is frequently revised or suspended at the executive's initiative.
iii. There is no legislative assembly, or there is one but it is called and dismissed at the executive's pleasure.
iv. The executive appoints a majority of members of any accountability group and can remove them at will.
v.   The legislature cannot initiate legislation or veto or suspend acts of the executive.
vi. Rule by decree is repeatedly used.

Rating of 5—Substantial limitations on executive authority. The executive has more effective authority that any accountability group, but is subject to substantial constraints by them.

Examples of evidence:
i.   A legislature or party council often modifies or defeats executive proposals for action.
ii. A council or legislature sometimes refuses funds to the executive.
iii. The accountability group makes important appointments to administrative posts.

Rating of 7—Executive parity or subordination. Accountability groups have effective authority equal to or greater than the executive in most areas of activity.

Examples of evidence:
i.   A legislature or party council of nobles initiates much or most important legislation.
ii. The executive (president, premier, king, cabinet, council) is chosen by the accountability group and is dependent on its continued support to remain in office (as in most parliamentary systems).
iii. In multiparty democracies, there is chronic "cabinet instability."

Previously a rubber stamp of the executive, these bodies have begun to assert their independence, and increasingly to perform their functions: overseeing the executive, representing citizens, making policies and enacting laws.

Legislative oversight is nowhere more important than over the budget. In developing and transition countries, the 1990s witnessed a trend toward legislative budget activism, reflecting the process of democratization. In Brazil, for example, Congress had historically played no significant role in the budget process, but constitutional changes in the 1980s gave it powers to modify the budget. In Africa, too, changes are occurring. South Africa and Uganda have passed Financial Adminis-

TABLE 3.1   Executive Constraints—2004 Polity IV Results for 60 Low-Income Countries

Executive Constraints Score	Country
High (score of 7) 9 countries	Bolivia, Comoros, India, Lesotho, Moldova, Mongolia, Nicaragua, Papua New Guinea, Solomon Islands
Medium-high (score of 5–6) 20 countries	Albania, Armenia, Bangladesh, Benin, Georgia, Ghana, Guyana, Honduras, Indonesia, Kenya, Malawi, Mali, Madagascar, Niger, Nigeria, Serbia and Montenegro, Senegal, Sierra Leone, Sri Lanka, Zambia
Medium-low (score of 3 or 4) 15 countries	Angola, Burkina Faso, Cambodia, Djibouti, Ethiopia, Guinea, Kyrgyz Republic, Lao PDR, Mauritania, Mozambique, Rwanda, Tanzania, Tajikistan, Uganda, Vietnam
Low (score of 1 or 2) 16 countries	Azerbaijan, Bhutan, Central African Republic, Cameroon, Chad, Rep. of Congo, Eritrea, Gambia, Guinea-Bissau, Nepal, Pakistan, Sudan, Togo, Uzbekistan, Yemen, Zimbabwe

Source: Marshall and Jaggers 2002.
Note: In 2004, Burundi, Democratic Republic of Congo, and Haiti are considered in "transition"; Bosnia and Herzegovina in a period of "interruption"; and Côte d'Ivoire in a period of "interregnum," during which there is a complete collapse of central political authority.

TABLE 3.2   The Quality of Some Direct Oversight Institutions in 25 Countries Summarized by Groups

	Legislature	National ombudsman	Supreme audit institutions	Anticorruption agency
OECD	79	83	98	85
Middle-income	66	81	92	68
IDA/BLEND	73	73	78	77

Source: www.globalintegrity.org.
Notes: Countries include: Australia, Germany, Italy, Japan, Portugal, United States, Argentina, Brazil, Guatemala, Mexico, Namibia, Panama, Philippines, Russian Federation, South Africa, Turkey, Ukraine, Venezuela, R.B, Ghana, India, Indonesia, Kenya, Nicaragua, Nigeria, Zimbabwe.
To get a score: each question within each category is scored on a 0–100 scale, using specific guidelines. The category score is the average of the scores for the individual questions.

tration or Budget Acts that give more influence to the legislature during budget formulation and approval. In Kenya, the parliament has flexed its muscles to the point that the budget dedicated to directly parliamentary-related salaries and expenditures comprises no less than 5 percent of the national budget. But, as box 3.3 illustrates, there still is a long way to go before developing country legislatures have adequate capability to perform their oversight function.

BOX 3.2   The Global Integrity Index as a Tool for Governance Monitoring

The GII, developed by the nongovernmental organization Global Integrity focuses on measurement of "the existence and effectiveness of mechanisms that prevent abuse of power and promote public integrity, and on the access that citizens have to their government." The GII has a nested design—with answers to more than 290 detailed questions providing the basis for estimating a variety of indicators at different levels of aggregation. This enables users to move from the more aggregated indicators to the most disaggregated, and thereby identify strengths and weaknesses. Country-specific scoring is done by a diverse panel of in-country experts, each operating individually to avoid "contamination by consensus," and with rigorous, "blind" peer review. In 2004 the index was estimated only for an initial 25 countries—6 OECD countries, 12 middle-income countries, and 7 IDA-eligible low-income countries. An additional benchmarking of 43 countries was undertaken in 2006. The box table below details the questions for 10 indicators that are most directly relevant to the dimensions of checks and balances highlighted for this report.

Some specific GII indicators

Indicators of transparency and civic participation

Civil society organizations—In law, do citizens have a right to form CSOs? Do they in practice? Can citizens organize into trade unions? In practice, do CSOs actively engage in public advocacy campaigns? Are civil society activists safe when working on corruption issues?

Access to information law—In law, do citizens have a right of access to information? In practice, is the right of access to information effective?

Freedom of the media—In law, is freedom of the media guaranteed? In law, is freedom of speech guaranteed? Are citizens able to form media entities? Are the media able to report on corruption? Are journalists safe when investigating corruption?

Indicators of justice and the rule of law

Judiciary—In law, is the independence of the judiciary guaranteed? Is the appointment process for high court judges effective? Can members of the judiciary be held accountable for their actions? Can citizens access the judicial system? In law, is there a program to protect witnesses in corruption cases? Are judges safe when adjudicating corruption cases?

Rule of law and access to justice—In practice, does the criminal justice process function according to the rule of law? In law, is there a general right of appeal? Are citizens protected from detention without trial? Are individual economic rights guaranteed?

Law enforcement—Is the law enforcement agency (that is, the police) effective? Can law enforcement officials be held accountable for their actions?

(continued)

> **BOX 3.2   The Global Integrity Index as a Tool for
> Governance Monitoring (continued)**

Indicators of direct oversight

Legislature—Can members of the legislature be held accountable (by the judiciary) for their actions? In law, are members of the legislature subject to prosecution? Are there regulations governing conflict of interest by members of the legislature? Can citizens access the asset disclosure records of members of the legislature? Can citizens access legislative processes and documents? Does the legislature have control of the budget? Can citizens access the national budgetary process?

National ombudsman—In law, is there a national ombudsman, public protector, or equivalent agency covering the entire public sector? Is the national ombudsman effective? Can citizens access the reports of the ombudsman?

Supreme audit institution   In law, is there a national supreme audit institution, auditor general, or equivalent agency covering the entire public sector? Is the supreme audit institution effective? Can citizens access reports of the supreme audit institution?

Anticorruption agency—In law, is there an agency (or group of agencies) with a legal mandate to address corruption? Is the main anticorruption agency effective? Can citizens access the main anticorruption agency?

Source: www.globalintegrity.org.

Legislative strengthening is best seen as a complement to related governance improvements involving civil society. Civil society organizations (CSOs) are sources of technical expertise and can provide specialized legislative committees with information about the effects of public policies and policy alternatives:

> ...*treating legislatures as self-contained entities that can be fixed by repairing internal mechanisms is unlikely to get very far. Rather,...it is more useful to think in terms of helping a society develop the capacity to enact laws that incorporate citizens' interests...[this means] working with many people and groups outside the legislature...*[47]

The internal workings of legislatures can nonetheless be important. In both Uganda and Kenya, a private-member bill established independent Parliamentary Commissions, joint parliamentary-executive boards that oversee the management and modernization of the legislature including, inter alia, the creation of a permanent, independent nonpartisan staff for parliament and the coordination of donor support to parliament. Such tasks require stronger institutional capacities in most parliaments in developing countries, where basic infrastructure is often missing.

> ## BOX 3.3 Legislative Oversight in Africa—A Work in Progress
>
> A recent study of legislatures in four African countries—Benin, Ghana, Kenya, and Senegal, identified large differences in their effectiveness. The Kenyan parliament emerged as the most independently assertive; the Ghanaian and Beninese legislatures were described as semi-independent (and certainly more independent as of 2002 than 10–15 years earlier); but the Senegalese legislature was judged to be almost entirely subservient to the executive.
>
> These variations in independence translated into variations in how parliamentarians allocated their time between policy-related and constituency-support activities, with the Kenyans most (and the Senegalese least) preoccupied with the former. But even in Kenya, there was only limited real engagement with the budgeting process (as distinct from other aspects of policy making), and even this engagement tended to focus narrowly on the implementation of spending commitments within the districts of individual members. Multiyear delays in the presentation of audits have led some parliamentarians to refer disparagingly to audit committees as the "postmortem committees."
>
> The study highlighted four factors shaping the effectiveness of legislatures. The first comprised the pull, evident in all countries, towards patronage-driven, "deliver the goods to constituents" behavior by legislators. The second comprised differences in formal rules, for example the extent to which they empower legislatures to shape the national budget. The third comprised differences in the pay and institutional resources available to parliamentarians—and hence the extent to which the parliamentarians perceive themselves to be dependent on executive favors to make ends meet. The final factor was the balance in the composition of representatives among "reformers," opportunistic "patronage seekers," and "incumbent authoritarians." The study posits a shift toward the former groups, and links this to a combination of generational change (with younger legislators being better educated and more globally connected), the rise of civic activism within urban elites, and the rise of multiparty democracy across Africa. Legislative performance is rooted in domestic social dynamics, and the authors conclude that "the modernization of the African legislature cannot be 'orchestrated from the outside.'"
>
> *Source:* Barkan, Adamolekun and Zhou 2004.

Steps are needed to give parliaments the ability to sustain their interventions, bring significant independent expertise to bear, and exercise effective leverage in their oversight activities. These might include making changes in internal rules to permit tougher scrutiny of key actions of the executive; establishing and strengthening of specialized committees (including those focused on budget, education, health, roads, rural development, and cross-cutting themes, such as poverty reduction); building linkages with CSOs and independent policy-advisory institutions; establishing well-paid research capabilities to serve parliament; and "putting their own house in order" to improve credibility—for example by establishing codes of conduct for members of parliaments, and by making campaign financing transparent, honest, and constrained.

Decentralization

Decentralization has a dual role in a national governance system. First, consistent with the theme of this chapter, democratic subnational governments can offer an important check and balance against central executive power. Second, as discussed further in chapter 4, subnational governments potentially have advantages in the provision of some local public services.

Decentralization often is driven by politics. Sierra Leone embarked on decentralization as a way of simultaneously building intergovernmental institutions, local government capacity, and bottom-up accountability. When that country's civil war ended in 2002, the government initiated a process of national consultation on decentralization. In February 2004, it enacted a progressive Local Government Act, establishing 19 local councils, which, over the period of 2004–8, will take over a large set of responsibilities and resources related to primary education, primary health, agriculture, feeder roads, water, and sanitation.

For decentralization to help reduce poverty, two sets of accountabilities need to work well. The first comprises downward accountability to local residents. As the 2004 World Development Report on improving service provision to the poor put it:[48]

> [Where] de-centralization is driven by a desire to move services administratively closer to the people…the assumption is that [it] works by enhancing citizens' voice in a way that leads to improved services… Voters make more use of information about local public goods in their voting decisions because such information is easier to come by and outcomes are more directly affected by local government actions. And political agents have greater credibility because of proximity to the community and reputations developed through social interaction over an extended period. But on both theoretical and empirical grounds this could go either way. The crucial question is always whether de-centralization increases accountability relative to its alternatives. If local governments are no more vulnerable to capture than the center is, de-centralization is likely to improve both efficiency and equity.

Downward accountability thus depends in part on local social structures. But it can also be nurtured—including by approaches to foster transparency and participation at local levels.

The second set of accountabilities comprises the arrangements that link central and local governments. These include the assignment of responsibilities for service provision (clarifying which services are assigned to local authorities, which are assigned to national authorities, and which involve complementary responsibilities for both local and central authorities); the allocation of fiscal resources (including some tax base for local authorities); and regulatory, fiduciary, and other forms of central oversight over local activity.

Clarifying these responsibilities in ways that gives each tier of government an incentive to perform its role efficiently is a deeply political and complex task. Decisions over the decentralization "rules of the game" involve a zero-sum contest between national and local politicians and bureaucracies over who controls resources and influence. The interplay between technical complexity and political jockeying can sometimes create difficulties. A comparative review of experiences in six East Asian countries (Cambodia, China, Indonesia, the Philippines, Thailand, and Vietnam) concluded that:[49]

> *the result [has been] a kind of "institutional limbo"...Whether by design or as a result of slippages in the implementation process, intergovernmental structures have substantial internal inconsistency. The functions of different levels of government overlap. Bottom-up accountability of locally elected bodies is dampened by top-down methods for appointing key officials. And the discretion given to local authorities in spending unconditional fiscal transfers is effectively curtailed by central government control over human resources.*

As the 2004 World Development Report concluded: [50] "Subnational authorities can be efficient providers and regulators of local services under the right institutional incentives and with clarity about who does what—and with what. But greater autonomy can also increase opportunistic behavior and create moral hazard, resulting in costs that diminish accountability and the benefits of decentralization. Good design, sound management, and constant adaptation by both central and subnational authorities are needed to make decentralization work."

The Middle Constellation—Justice and the Rule of Law

This section will define what is meant by "justice reform and the rule of law," will examine some approaches to monitoring, and will highlight some emerging lessons from efforts at reform.

Defining

Justice sector reform and promoting the rule of law have emerged as key goals of development policy. The justice sector covers a vast array of institutions, issues, and functions. In the broadest terms, it can be defined as the institutions and processes by which laws are devised and enforced. It includes, for instance, legal services and their providers (e.g. lawyers and paralegals), police, prosecutors, the judiciary, courts and their officials, other institutions that resolve disputes, and institutions that execute judgments. At the same time, the justice sector fulfills certain essential functions, such as, safety and security, resolving disputes, and providing checks and balances on the use of state power. The specific types of issues that the justice sector addresses include, in no particular order: civil disputes (property, contract, and land), business and corporate regulation (corporate transactions, financial governance, insolvency), criminal law, administrative law, human rights and constitutional redress, citizenship and migration, and so on.

Additionally, a well-functioning justice sector is expected to reflect certain basic qualities, most notably, the rule of law. Indeed, the term rule of law is sometimes seen as synonymous with, or used as a proxy for, a well-functioning justice sector. Yet, as with the justice sector generally, there is no shortage of conceptions as to what the rule of law is said to entail[51] (see box 3.4). Both the rule of law and justice reform have been defined broadly with reference to their essential role in ensuring democracy and human rights, or narrowly—for example with reference to their impact on predictability for business processes and investment climate. The difference in priority and definition will have a direct impact on which reform efforts are prioritized to improve the functioning of the justice sector and the rule of law and, in turn, what should be measured.

Monitoring

There already exist a number of both broad and specific indicators on rule of law issues. Most of them, however, are not aimed specifically at the rule of law, and only incorporate a section on it, as part of a broader focus or theme. Others, while focusing on justice and rule of law issues, focus on specific processes or institutions and do not seek an overall view of the state of the rule of law.

BOX 3.4   Common Definitions of the "Rule of Law"

Formal definitions look to the presence or absence of specific, observable criteria of the law or the legal system. These explicit standards stand as benchmarks for the functioning of the rule of law. For example, the following criteria have been listed as basic standards: generality, notice or publicity, nonretroactivity, clarity, noncontradictoriness, conformability, stability, and congruence between the rules and the pattern of their enforcement.[52] Reform efforts aimed at improving the rule of law that reflect a more formal definition would include, for instance, efforts to redraft and publish legislation. The advantage of a formal definition is that, once the criteria have been identified, it provides ostensibly objective criteria for gauging whether the rule of law exists. The weakness of the formal definition is precisely that it tends to reflect more the "law on the books" than experiences of "law in action."

Substantive definitions articulate the rule of law according to moral or legal goods, such as ensuring "justice," "equality," or "fairness." By focusing on outcomes, a substantive definition has the advantage of not reducing the rule of law to a closed- or open-ended set of formal criteria, which may not entirely translate into those outcomes. But substantive definitions are more subjective and vague than their formal counterparts and, accordingly, do not lend themselves to being the immediate goal of reform efforts.

Functional definitions focus on how well the law and legal system perform some function. Thus, this definition is centered on outcomes, but lists them in more concrete, individuated terms; for instance, constraint on government discretion or making legal decisions predictable. The main drawback of the functional conception is that there is no guarantee that achievement of a particular functional rule of law goal would translate into a good thing. (For instance, legal decisions may be predictable, as a functional outcome, yet substantively unjust).

Two sets of broad indicators that make global comparisons among countries are the KK Rule of Law aggregate indicator, and the Property Rights and Rule-based Governance CPIA criterion. The KK Rule of Law indicator "aggregates data from multiple sources about outcomes of a functioning justice sector (control of the incidence of crime), more formal functional characteristics of the judiciary (effectiveness and predictability), and a particular function of a justice system (its ability to enforce contracts)."[53] The CPIA-rules indicator focuses primarily on the extent to which the legal system facilitates private economic activity, but also looks at broad outcomes (safety), specific outcomes and functions (provision of business licenses, contract enforcement), and formal characteristics of the system. The correlation between the two indicators is 0.83.

Table 3.3 uses the two aggregate indicators to distinguish among three groups of countries. The top group comprises 12 countries that are both in the top third of the KK rankings for the indicator, and have a CPIA-rules score of 3.5 or above. The bottom group comprises 23 countries that are in the bottom third for KK, and

TABLE 3.3   KK Rule of Law 2004, Adjusted for CPIA-Rules for 66 Low-Income Aid-Recipient Countries

	In relevant third (with 95% certainty)	In relevant third (with less than 95 % certainty)	
Overall Top Third	Bhutan, Ghana, India, Lesotho, Malawi, Senegal, Sri Lanka	Armenia, Honduras **With 95 % certainty top half:** Madagascar, Mali, Tanzania	
Overall Middle (a)	Mongolia	Djibouti, Guyana, Mozambique, São Tomé and Principe, Vietnam, Benin, Bolivia, Gambia, Zambia	
Overall Middle (b)	Azerbaijan	**Could be in bottom third:** Bangladesh, Cambodia, Eritrea, Ethiopia, Georgia,* Indonesia, Kenya, Niger, Rwanda	**Could be in top third:** Albania, Bosnia and Herzegovina, Burkina Faso, Mauritania, Moldova*, Nepal, Nicaragua, Pakistan, Papua New Guinea, Serbia and Montenegro, Uganda*
Overall Middle (c)		Solomon Islands **In bottom half (with 95 % certainty):** Lao PDR	
Overall Bottom Third	Angola, Burundi, Central African Republic, Congo Dem. Rep. of, Haiti, Côte d'Ivoire, Nigeria, Sudan, Uzbekistan, Zimbabwe	Comoros, Guinea, Kyrgyz Republic, Sierra Leone, Togo **In bottom half (with 95 % certainty):** Cameroon, Chad, Congo Rep. of, Guinea-Bissau, Tajikistan, Yemen Republic of	

Source: Adapted by author from Kaufmann, Kraay, and Mastruzzi (2005).
(a) Top third in KK Rule of Law (RoL), CPIA-rules below 3.5.
(b) KK and RoL consistent as to the "middle."
(c) Bottom third in KK Rule of Law; CPIA-rules 3.0 or above.
* Country is in the middle third with respect to the KK score and in the top group of the IDA sample with respect to the CPIA 12-rules score in 2004.

score below 3.0 on CPIA-rules. The intermediate group comprises countries with "middling" scores on one or both indicators. Similar to the patterns evident in table 1.3 and table 3.6, with the large margins of error only 20 of the 66 countries can be attributed to their group with at least 95 percent certainty.

As with other governance subsystems, efforts are underway to develop specific, actionable indicators for justice and the rule of law. Four sets of narrow indicators are noteworthy. The first two comprise the DB and ICS surveys introduced in chapter 1. Both surveys include indicators that can be used to monitor the performance of the justice system relevant to specific features of the business environment. (See annex table 1.2 for specific indicators relevant to the justice system).

The second two sets of disaggregated, actionable indicators focus more directly on the operation of the justice system itself. One comprises the GII, introduced in box 3.2. Table 3.4 summarizes the scores for three GII subindicators that most directly monitor the quality of the justice system for the 25 OECD, middle- and low-income countries for which it has so far been estimated. The final set, described in box 3.5, focuses on the internal efficiency of the judicial system. It has so far been used only for the 40 member states of the Council of Europe.

Reforming

So far, actionable indicators are not well enough developed to guide lesson learning about what makes for an effective reform of the justice system and how to sequence reforms. Lessons are being gleaned from monitoring and evaluations of specific projects, from observations and comparisons of reform efforts across countries, and from studies on specific aspects of rule of law. Consistent with the general thrust of the framework for assessing national governance used in this report, one key general theme is the importance of looking beyond specific legal deficiencies and specific gaps in the capacities and infrastructures of the formal justice system, and focusing on the incentives for the various players. As one observer put it:

> In order for the judiciary to perform the dispute resolution and credibility conferring functions generally assigned to it, all relevant parties must have appropriate incentives. Individuals must have an incentive to rely on the courts to adjudicate their disputes rather than relying on alternative, socially

TABLE 3.4   The Quality of Some Attributes of the Justice System in 25 Countries (by group)

	Judiciary	Rule of law and access to justice	Law enforcement
OECD	79	93	90
Middle-income	71	74	63
IDA/BLEND	58	72	59

Source: www.globalintegrity.org.
Note: Countries as in Table 3.2.

BOX 3.5   Indicators of the Efficiency of Judicial Processes

The European Commission for the Efficiency of Justice (CEPEJ) has launched two indicator initiatives. One is a *Checklist on Time Management in the Courts*, which is aimed at helping to collect information as to the duration of judicial proceedings.[54] The other initiative is the *Pilot Scheme for Evaluating Judicial Systems*, launched in 2004. This questionnaire probes the total amount of the budget covering the operation of the courts, legal aid, and prosecution. It examines legal aid, access to courts, and citizen confidence in the justice system. Other sections look at: (i) the organization of the court system, its functioning and monitoring and evaluation; (ii) aspects required for a fair trial, including fundamental principles, timeframes of proceedings, civil and administrative, as well as criminal cases; (iii) the career of judges and prosecutors, including appointment, salary, training, and disciplinary procedures, (iv) lawyers, including number in the country, organization of the profession, qualifications, fees, and complaints and disciplinary procedures; (v) alternative dispute resolution; and (vi) enforcement of court decisions.

*Sources:*http://www.coe.int/T/E/Legal_Affairs/Legal_cooperation/Operation_of_justice/Efficiency_of_justice/Presentation, http://www.coe.int/T/E/Legal_Affairs/Legal_co-operation/Operation_of_justice/Efficiency_of_justice/ Documents/.

---

undesirable dispute resolution mechanism or forgoing certain transactions altogether. Those with the power to disregard judicial decisions or to subvert judicial independence must have an incentive to refrain from such activities, and the judges themselves must have an incentive to carry out the functions assigned to them.[55]

At a more detailed level, three sets of hypotheses seem to be emerging as useful guides to the design of justice reform.

First is the benefit of working simultaneously on independence and accountability. Early efforts to increase independence of courts tended to focus on how judges are selected and evaluated, and their capacity to deliberate and decide cases without undue influence from other branches of government or pressure from people or factors not at issue in the case at hand. Accountability of judges, particularly to the public—by means such as making judicial budgets and court statistics transparent, requiring declaration of assets and income by judges and court officials, reinforcing management structures and processes to control corruption, and so forth—was sometimes not given as much emphasis as judicial independence. This focus on independence at the expense of accountability has occurred in Europe and Central Asia[56] and Latin American and the Caribbean,[57] and is of concern, given that citizens' greatest complaints about courts tend to focus first on corruption and second on delay, neither of which are likely to improve substantially without greater judicial accountability.

Second, reforms that seek to overhaul the way justice systems operate will only stick if they deliberately strengthen the management of the reform process. Profound institutional change requires professional change management at the planning and implementation stages. This is pointed out quite clearly in studies by the Centro de Estudios de Justicia de las Americas of the criminal justice reform processes in many countries of Latin America, in which bold attempts to replace written processes with oral hearings and trials suffered backsliding in the absence of improved management of the institutions involved.

Third, if one is seeking to increase the amount or quality of justice for the average citizen, it is necessary to look at both formal and informal justice systems. Most World Bank projects, and many of the justice reform projects of major donors, focus on improving the administration of justice through formal institutions—courts, prosecutors' offices, ministries of justice, and so on. Assistance has also been provided to legal aid institutions, and major donors have supported development of alternative dispute resolution mechanisms such as mediation and arbitration, though often as a recognized part of a formal proceeding. The role of informal, local justice systems, which in some countries govern as much as 95 percent of the population, have only recently begun to receive more attention. The most recent "pro-poor" judicial reform initiatives focus not on trying to externally engineer greater "compatibility" between formal and customary systems, but on creating new mediating institutions, wherein actors from both realms can meet, following simple, transparent, mutually agreed-upon, and accountable rules to craft new arrangements that both sides can own and enforce. Rather than being stand-alone "judicial reform" projects, these initiatives are appended on to or incorporated into more mainstream development projects, seeking to use the incentives associated with accessing material resources for roads, schools, and so forth, as a basis for establishing new precedents and procedures for decision making and priority setting. The Bank is now studying whether these approaches help participants find more constructive solutions to local-level conflict, and what mechanisms tend to achieve such positive outcomes and potentially avoid or minimize negative outcomes.[58]

But even as these lessons begin to emerge, one critical gap remains: We don't know much about what types of reform are most effective in particular country circumstances (for example, post-conflict, middle income).

The Outer Constellation—Transparency and Voice

Citizen engagement, underpinned by access to high-quality information, forms the outermost, and possibly the most important, element of a national system of checks and balances. Transparency was highlighted in chapter 1 as a critical part of good governance, chapter 2 examined how it supports public financial and administrative systems, and chapter 4 will focus on how it can buttress the service provision front line. This chapter complements the others by focusing on the potential of transparency to encourage a virtuous circle of accountability.

Figure 3.2 depicts the "virtuous circle of transparency" in a way that highlights the links between the provision of information and state responsiveness. Information reveals the actions of policy makers; this facilitates evaluation and monitoring; activism rises, and with it the level of public debate. Policy becomes more contestable, and citizens are motivated by the possibility of holding the government accountable. Communication with the government becomes a two-way flow, generating further demands for more reliable information. The virtuous circle is completed as government practices become more open and more responsive to citizens.

Two factors are needed for this process to work well. One is the production and dissemination of good-quality information. The other involves strengthening capacity for analysis, interpretation, debate, and advocacy within civil society. The next two subsections consider each in turn. The subsequent subsection will examine some options for monitoring country performance vis-à-vis transparency and voice.

The Supply and Dissemination of Information

The emergence of global norms for data—described in box 3.6—brings an increasingly important global dimension to the production of high-quality information. There is, as yet, no agreed-upon single measure of capacity to produce good-quality public statistics, but work carried out as part of IDA 14 provides a basis for monitoring changes in the performance of statistical systems. Data are compiled annually on three key dimensions of capacity: statistical *practice,* data *collection,* and indicator *availability.* The three are combined to generate overall indicators for

FIGURE 3.2 The Virtuous Circle of Transparency—from Disclosure to Responsiveness

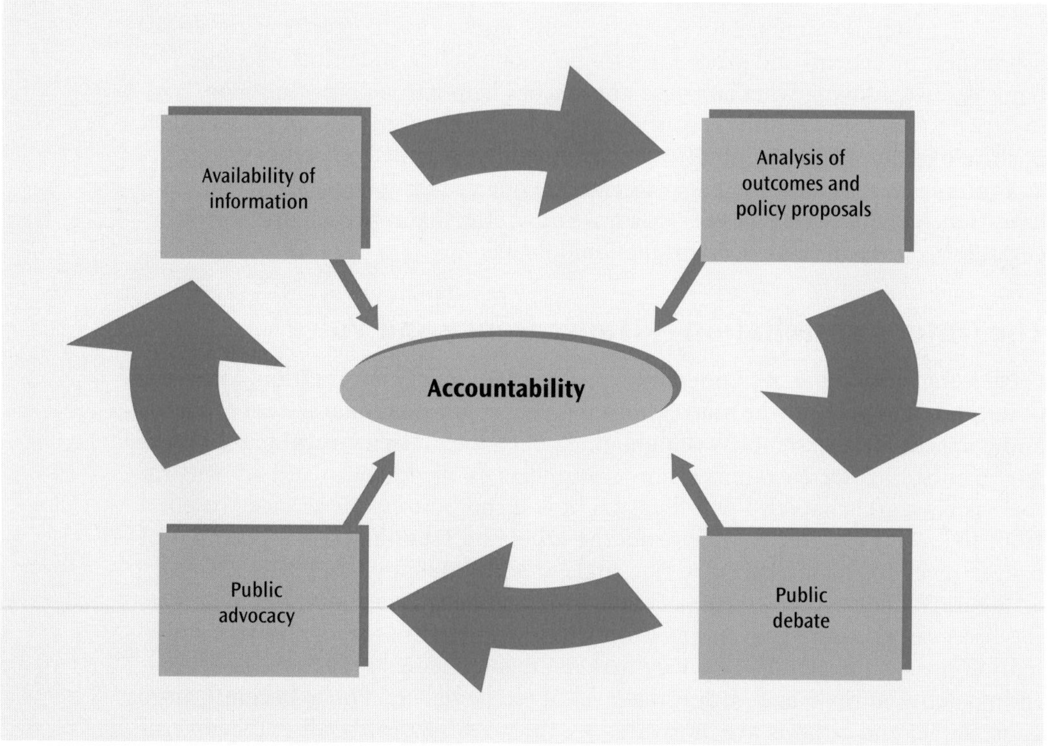

Source: World Bank 2006, 160.

each dimension, and to produce a single overall indicator. This measure paints a worrying picture of statistical capacity (figure 3.3). Statistical "practice" is the dimension of capacity that focuses on the extent to which countries engage in the collection of primary data. (Statistical availability includes proxy data or simulation results.) As the low average score in figure 3.3 for "practice" signals, many IDA countries lack the ability to provide basic statistics on a regular basis, resulting in a vicious cycle—limited, poor-quality data reduce demand for data and lowers interest in supporting data collection. Capacity has been increasing slowly, if at all, in most poor countries. Especially in the poorest, the impact of projects to strengthen statistical capacity has often been disappointing. Investments are usually not sustained, often because of the piecemeal, short-term nature of projects.

The Marrakech Action Plan for Statistics (MAPS), an international response to meeting the data challenges of monitoring the MDGs, adopts a more comprehensive, country-led approach. The objective of the action plan for statistics is to help all developing countries to either implement or prepare a longer-term national statistical development plan by the end of 2006. It is too early to assess the effectiveness of the approach, but initial experience suggests that it can be effective and that improvements can be achieved and maintained. Lessons so far include the need to focus on both long-term institutional reform, as well as shorter-term data availability, and to build demand for statistics, as well as collecting more data. In the short

FIGURE 3.3 Measuring Country Statistical Capacity: IBRD, IDA, and IDA-Africa, 1999–2005

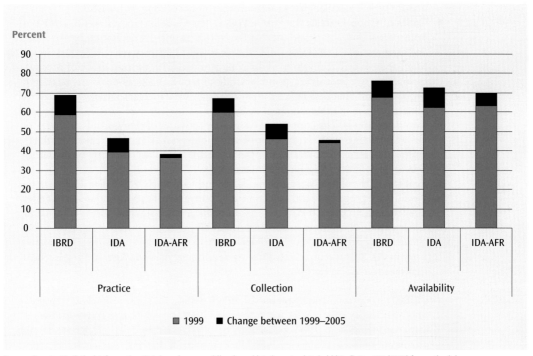

Source: Country Statistical Information Database (www.worldbank.org/data/countrydata/csid.html). See IDA (2004) for methodology.

BOX 3.6 Global Norms for Collection and Publication of Economic and Social Data

Recent initiatives by international agencies, including the IMF and World Bank, have begun to put in place a framework of internationally accepted norms for the collection and publication of basic economic and social data. These can serve as benchmarks for capacity building. The Standards and Codes initiative aims to enhance the public availability of reliable, timely, and comprehensive statistics, and to disseminate good practices in monetary, financial, and fiscal policy transparency:

- **Special Data Dissemination Standard (SDDS).** Created in 1996, the SDDS is a voluntary standard whose subscribers—countries with market access or seeking it—commit to meeting internationally accepted levels of data coverage, frequency, and timeliness. SDDS subscribers provide information about their data dissemination practices for posting on the Dissemination Standards Bulletin Board (DSBB) at http://dsbb.imf.org, and are required to maintain an internet web site that contains the actual data. SDDS subscribers began disseminating prescribed data on external debt in September 2003.
- **General Data Dissemination System (GDDS).** For countries that do not have market access, the GDDS provides a detailed framework that promotes the use of internationally accepted methodological principles, the adoption of rigorous compilation practices, and ways in which the professionalism of national statistical agencies can be enhanced. The 79 IMF members participating in the GDDS at the end of April 2005 provide metadata describing their data compilation and dissemination practices, as well as detailed plans for improvement for posting on the DSBB
- **Codes of Good Practice for Public Policy.** The Code of Good Practices in Fiscal Transparency sets out standards for the collection and dissemination of fiscal data and information. The Guide on Resource Revenue Transparency supplements the Manual on Fiscal Transparency for countries with a significant share of revenues from extractive industries. And the Code of Good Practices on Transparency in Monetary and Financial Policies identifies desirable data transparency practices for central banks and other financial agencies.
- **Corporate Sector.** The corporate governance activities of the World Bank focus on the rights and equitable treatment of shareholders, the treatment of stakeholders, disclosure and transparency, and the duties of board members by applying the OECD Principles of Corporate Governance.
- **Reports on the Observance of Standards and Codes (ROSCs).** The IMF and the World Bank prepare reports of countries' observance of these standards and codes. As of the end of April 2005, ROSC assessments and updates had been completed for about two-thirds of the membership. About 70 percent of these reports have subsequently been published. Participation rates vary substantially across regions, ranging from under 30 percent of members in developing Asia to close to 90 percent in Central and Eastern Europe.

The OECD has promulgated standards and guidelines that aim to improve the quality and availability of statistics for its member countries. **The Extractive Industries' Transparency Initiative (EITI)** promotes the publication by both governments and companies of public revenues arising from extractive industries.

term, the focus may need to be on dealing with the imbalances between supply and demand for data to build support and break out of the vicious cycle of low supply and low demand for data.

Disclosure is the critical step that makes information transparent—and turns it into a potent tool for civic accountability. All governments routinely disclose reams of information, including selective information aimed at shaping public opinion. Most democratic societies have some basic standards of disclosure—publication of judicial decisions, or the records of parliamentary debates, for example.

More recently, however, global changes in politics, technology, and values have converged to provide a powerful impetus for efforts to strengthen the transparency of governance systems. Societal and political trends, including higher levels of literacy and democratization, have raised expectations of enhanced transparency and accountability, as evidenced by international campaigns to measure and assess corruption (Transparency International), encourage publication of key data (The "Publish What You Pay" and Extractive Industries Transparency Initiatives), and promote freedom of information laws. The rise of NGOs continues to strengthen the capacity of civil society, including by raising financial resources and sharing technical knowledge across borders. Advances in information and communication technologies have substantially reduced the costs and complexities of gathering, processing, and publishing large quantities of data, while significantly enhancing accessibility of information posted on Web sites.

The values dimension of the push for transparency is articulated by Amartya Sen, who notes that successful development is underpinned by the respect of a wide range of rights, including transparency guarantees. These play instrumental roles in institutions or capabilities that are necessary to empower people, acting singly or as a group, to raise their own welfare.[59] In accordance with this view, access to information is enshrined as a fundamental human right in the Declaration of Human Rights. It is also a principle in the Declaration of Principles on Freedom of Expression by the Inter-American Commission on Human Rights,[60] and a basic requirement in a number of international treaties (such as World Trade Organization agreements and North America Free Trade Agreement). The Inter-American Court of Human Rights has stated that the "concept of public order in a democratic society requires the guarantee of the widest possible circulation of news, ideas and opinions as well as the widest access to information by society as a whole."[61]

This global sea change is reflected in the growing number of countries that have adopted freedom of information laws[62]—over 50 as of the end of 2004, with efforts underway in an additional 30. The trend is spreading worldwide: in Asia, nearly a dozen countries have either adopted laws or are on the brink of doing so. In South and Central America and the Caribbean, half a dozen countries have adopted laws and nearly a dozen more are currently considering them. South Africa enacted a wide-reaching law in 2001, and many countries in southern and central Africa, mostly members of the Commonwealth, are following its lead. Box 3.7 summarizes the nine principles that generally underpin freedom of information (FOI) laws.

Guaranteeing in law the right to access information is a way of signaling government's commitment to transparency. Such a law can be an important tool in building democratic attitudes and enhancing trust in institutions. However, the enactment of an FOI law is only the beginning. To be of any use, it must be implemented and public institutions must change their internal cultures. Perseverance of civil society is therefore crucial, with civil society groups such as the press, ombudsmen, and NGOs playing a key role in the promotion and adoption of freedom of information laws, and in ensuring that the laws are effectively implemented.

Enhancing Capacity for the Effective Use of Information by Civil Society

Engaged civil society emerges as crucial to a well-functioning governance system. How can greater capacity and engagement be facilitated in the collective processes of public policy formulation and implementation? One set of options, considered in chapter 4, focuses on engagement close to the service provision front line. The focus here is on facilitating more—and higher-quality—engagement upstream. Interventions at three radically different levels illustrate the variety of entry points through which this might be attempted.

The first level comprises specific efforts to strengthen the capacity for economic and policy discourse outside of government. A successful, longstanding effort in sub-Saharan Africa illustrates how this can be done. The effort involved support for both the African Economic Research Consortium (AERC), which has sought to strengthen economics education and research, and for the Africa Capacity Building Foundation (ACBF), which has helped to create autonomous policy think tanks

---

BOX 3.7   The Principles That Generally Underpin Freedom of Information Laws

1. **Maximum disclosure.** Freedom of information legislation should be guided by the principle of maximum disclosure.
2. **Obligation to publish.** Public bodies should be under an obligation to publish key information.
3. **Promotion of open government.** Public bodies must actively promote open government.
4. **Limited scope of exceptions.** Exceptions should be clearly and narrowly drawn and subject to strict "harm" and "public interest" tests.
5. **Process to facilitate access.** Requests for information should be processed rapidly and fairly, and an independent review of any refusal should be available.
6. **Costs.** Individuals should not be deterred from making requests for information by excessive costs.
7. **Open meetings.** Meetings of public bodies should be open to the public.
8. **Disclosure takes precedence.** Laws that are inconsistent with the principle of maximum disclosure should be amended or repealed.
9. **Protection for whistleblowers.** Individuals who release information on wrongdoing must be protected.

Source: Mendel 2004.

---

since 1993. It helped set up these think tanks in close to 20 countries, with the vast majority governed by an independent, politically nonpartisan, and highly respected board of directors. Many of them have won a visible and highly credible voice in their country's policy discourse via a combination of solid research, effective outreach, a reputation for delivering high-quality commissioned analytical work, plus some policy work for government. While causality cannot, of course, be directly attributed, the strengthening of this network has coincided with not only a sharp rise in the quality of economic policy discourse in many African countries, but also with radical improvements in economic policy itself. However, the tension between the role of these think tanks as independent voices in the policy discourse and their pressure to become financially viable must be noted. So far, the tension has been resolved via donor and foundation funding, but the combination of the relatively short-term (typically two- to four-year) horizon of these commitments, and the ever-present drumbeat of pressure from donors that their recipients find alternative sources of financing, implies that even the substantial gains that have been made are at risk.

The second level comprises the effort to orchestrate participatory policy formulation processes that explicitly engage civil society. The Poverty Reduction Strategy is an obvious example. The PRS process marked a departure from the earlier practice of donors and international financial institutions of focusing narrowly on the executive, and has sought to more directly engage citizens and their elected representatives. A recent progress review suggests some advancement on this front (table 3.5), but shows that engagement is well developed in only a minority of countries. Even so, the PRS has proven to be a valuable tool for crowding civil society more systematically into the policy discourse in countries as diverse as Rwanda, Cameroon, and Vietnam.

- *Rwanda's* PRS process has complemented and helped deepen dialogue initiated through the National Unity and Reconciliation Commission (NURC), set up to promote peace, tolerance, and respect following the 1994 genocide. There is easy public access to the PRS, including a summary in Kinyarwanda, and to fiscal data, as well as the emergence of some leading CSOs vocal on poverty issues. Participatory surveys and stakeholder seminars have been conducted by the Poverty Observatory, a strategic planning and monitoring directorate charged with monitoring PRS implementation. Efforts are underway to merge dialogue held by the NURC with that conducted by the Poverty Observatory. The result is that the development debate is being consolidated with stronger analytical underpinnings.
- *Vietnam* produces a Socio-Economic Development Plan (SEDP) every five years. The SEDP typically has been prepared by central government agencies with little consultation outside of the Communist Party. Subsequent to the finalization of the 2001–5 SEDP, the government embarked on developing a PRS—the Comprehensive Poverty Reduction and Growth Strategy (CPRGS)—together with local experts and researchers, as well as international and local CSOs. The existence of parallel processes and strategies has caused some confusion on the reference point for policy makers, but has provoked unprecedented lively debate

TABLE 3.5   Participation in the PRS, 2005

| | | Civil Society Participation | | |
		Little action	Action underway	Well developed
Parliamentary Involvement	Well developed	Bhutan, Djibouti, Lao PDR, Tajikistan	Bosnia and Herzegovina, Burkina Faso, Cambodia, Guinea, Honduras, Madagascar, Mali, Mauritania, Moldova, Mozambique, Timor-Leste	Ghana, Rwanda, Uganda
	Action underway	Azerbaijan, Benin, Congo, Rep. of, Pakistan	Armenia, Burundi, Cape Verde, Ethiopia, Kyrgyz Republic, Liberia, Mongolia, Niger, Serbia and Montenegro, Yemen, Zambia	Tanzania, Vietnam
	Little action	Central African Republic, Congo, Dem. Rep. of, Côte d'Ivoire, Dominica, Guinea-Bissau, Nepal, São Tomé and Principe, Sri Lanka, Sudan	Albania, Bangladesh, Bolivia, Chad, Gambia, Georgia, Guyana, Haiti, Kenya, Lesotho, Malawi, Nicaragua, Senegal, Sierra Leone	Cameroon

Source: World Bank 2005a.

on policy directions in the National Assembly. In preparing the 2006–10 SEDP, the government has committed to emulate the participatory approach to planning that characterized the preparation of the CPRGS.

■ *Cameroon's* PRS has resulted in greater access to information and empowered civil society to conduct dialogue with the government and development partners on programming, budgeting, and monitoring of poverty-oriented policies. Development Committees—longstanding participatory bodies composed of civil society and private sector representatives at the level of districts, divisions and provinces—were reactivated during the formulation of the *Document de Stratégie de Réduction de la Pauvreté,* Cameroon's PRS, and are making investment proposals according to community needs. CSOs also participate in a committee to monitor allocation of HIPC resources and, together with religious organizations, have established a *Forum Cameroun* to identify a common platform on strategies to reduce poverty.

The third level comprises the institutional arrangements to enable the civic realm to function effectively—exemplified here by the governance arrangements for an independent media. Independent media is a crucial pillar of good governance, and a critical link in the accountability chain between the government and the governed—disseminating information about government policies and actions, monitoring government functions, and providing a check on the exercise of authority. Investigative journalists increase the likelihood of detection of corruption and punitive action, thus fostering good governance. Mass media also functions as a channel of citizen voice, thus influencing government policies and actions to be more relevant and responsive to citizen preferences.

Keys to the media's ability to perform these roles effectively are the structure of the media industry and the regulatory environment within which it functions:

- State ownership creates obvious constraints to media independence and its ability to be an independent monitor of government functions. A recent survey of 97 countries found that the state controls over 60 percent of TV stations and 29 percent of newspapers, and found that the extent of state ownership of media institutions was negatively correlated with key social indicators such as health and education, as well as citizens' rights and security of property.
- Even when the media are not directly controlled by the state, restrictive regulatory environments—especially restrictions on entering broadcasting markets, high license fees, restrictions on freedom of expression in the form of repressive defamation laws, and the absence of legal underpinnings for freedom of information create adverse conditions for effective media oversight.
- Private control of media institutions is no panacea. Media ownership tends to be very highly concentrated, with large families and conglomerates controlling the bulk of media outlets. The commercial interests of owners, and the search for advertising revenue, all too frequently result in private media championing causes that are tied to their commercial interests rather than the largest public good. Financial constraints also can hamper the effectiveness of the media, via technology and capacity gaps, and by keeping journalist wages low, thus providing ready inducements for corruption.

Yet for all of these limitations, in many developing countries the media are vibrant, and of good quality. As box 3.8 underscores, this can be a potent development asset.

Monitoring Transparency and Voice

One broad and one narrow set of indicators are used in this subsection to monitor transparency and voice (TV). The broad indicator captures the overall TV environment—including the human rights and political governance dimensions. The narrow indicator focuses more directly on those aspects of transparency most directly relevant for achieving the MDGs.

BOX 3.8   How Media Access Can Influence Development Outcomes

A variety of studies have documented the link between better-informed citizens and better-performing governments. Besley and Burgess (2002) show that state governments in India were far more responsive to food crises in those states that had high newspaper circulation than in those that did not. Adserá, Boix, and Payne (2003) find, similarly, that corruption is significantly lower in countries with high newspaper circulation. And Strömberg (2004) finds for the United States that households with radios during the Great Depression were much more likely to benefit from relief efforts than households that lacked them.[63]

Two broad indicators were considered for this report—the aggregate Kaufmann-Kraay (KK) "voice and accountability" (VA) indicator, and a related indicator that focuses more narrowly on transparency. Table 3.6 reports the better-established "voice and accountability" indicator. [At 0.88 the correlation between the VA and the transparency indicators is high.[64]] The indicator is estimated from 19 separate disaggregated sources—each of which focuses on a specific aspect of VA. KK note that these include[65] "a number of indicators measuring various aspects of the political process, civil liberties and political rights. These indicators measure the extent to which citizens are able to participate in the selection of governments. We also include indicators measuring the independence of the media, which serves an important role in monitoring those in authority and holding them accountable for their actions."

Table 3.6 reports the distribution of the sample of 66 IDA-eligible countries across three groups, distinguishing among countries according to whether one can be at least 95 percent confident, using a two-tailed test, that they indeed fall into the category in which they are located. As with all governance measures, the indicator provides some useful benchmarking, but only for a minority of countries is it possible to assert with confidence that their environment for voice and accountability is relatively strong or relatively weak.

If we locate high- and middle-income countries in the KK VA sample using the same cutoff points as for the 66-country-IDA-eligible sample, a considerable number fall below table 3.6's top-third group. While all of the high-income OECD member countries are significantly above the top third cutoff point for the 66-country sample, six non-OECD high-income countries are located below this cutoff point. Of 77 middle-income countries, 30 rank below the top-third cutoff point, and 16 of these score low enough to be in the bottom third of the 66-country sample.

TABLE 3.6   KK Voice and Accountability 2004, IDA and Blend Countries

	In relevant third (with 95% certainty)	In relevant third (with less than 95% certainty)	
Top third	Benin, Ghana, India, Lesotho, Mali, Mongolia, São Tomé and Principe, Senegal, Serbia and Montenegro	**In top half (with 95% certainty):** Albania, Bolivia , Bosnia and Herzegovina, Comoros, Guyana, Honduras, Madagascar , Mozambique, Nicaragua , Níger, Papua New Guinea, Solomon Islands	
Middle third	Armenia, Bangladesh, Gambia, Guinea-Bissau, Indonesia, Malawi, Moldova, Nigeria, Sierra Leone, Uganda	**Could be in bottom third:** Azerbaijan, Cambodia, Congo, Djibouti, Nepal, Yemen, Republic of	**Could be in top third:** Burkina Faso, Georgia, Kenya, Sri Lanka, Tanzania, Zambia
Bottom third	Congo, Dem. Rep. of, Côte d'Ivoire, Eritrea, Haiti, Lao PDR, Pakistan, Sudan, Uzbekistan, Vietnam, Zimbabwe	**In bottom half (with 95% certainty):** Angola, Bhutan, Burundi, Cameroon, Central African Republic, Chad, Ethiopia, Guinea, Kyrgyz Republic, Mauritania, Rwanda, Tajikistan, Togo	

Source: Kaufmann, Kray, and Mastruzzi 2005.

The specific indicators are taken from the GII. The GII includes multiple subindicators on issues ranging from the environment for civil society organization and the media, to freedom of information laws. Table 3.7 reports the scores for three narrowly focused GII subindicators, which measure facets of the environment for transparency and civic participation for 26 OECD, middle- and low-income countries. Low-income countries lag, especially in the right of access to information.

The Challenge of Sequencing Checks and Balances and Bureaucracy Reforms

This final section brings together some of the individual governance measures examined in this and the previous chapter to pose a complex question: how to engage countries with an uneven mix of governance strengths and weaknesses? This is a somewhat different problem from the question of how to engage with countries with severe, all-around governance weaknesses, in part because the uneven mix may reflect turnaround cases rather than stable, clientelistic equilibria.

Trajectories of Change

Table 3.9 applies the governance indicators used in earlier sections to identify 28 countries that rate well in the quality of either their bureaucracies or their checks-and-balances institutions. (The Appendix to this volume provides further disaggregated detail.) While 10 countries rate well in both areas, performance across the remaining countries is uneven. Ten countries (Rwanda and Vietnam, for example) have relatively capable public bureaucracies, but less strong checks-and-balances institutions. And the pattern is reversed in the other eight countries (Albania and Lesotho, for instance), where relatively stronger indicators for checks and balances are not matched by correspondingly capable public bureaucracies. (As annex 3.1 details, by taking a unified look at the measures laid out in this chapter, countries also differ in the relative strengths of different checks-and-balances institutions.) Over the long term, strong checks-and-balances institutions limit the risk of reversals and are key to sustainable development. Yet, while in some countries strengthening of the range of checks-and-balances institutions is part of the broader trajectory of governance and development gains, as the table shows, in others the change process is more uneven.

TABLE 3.7 Global Integrity Index—Transparency and Civic Participation (by group)

	Civil society organizations	Access to information law	Freedom of the media
OECD countries	95	87	91
Middle-income countries	88	60	74
Low-income countries	82	41	79

Source: www.globalintegrity.org.

TABLE 3.8   State Capacity and State Accountability

	Quality of checks-and-balances institutions	
	Medium or Low	Higher
Higher	10 countries (Azerbaijan, Bhutan, Burkina Faso, Ethiopia, Indonesia, Pakistan, Rwanda, Tanzania, Uganda, Vietnam)	10 countries (Armenia, Benin, Bolivia, Ghana, Honduras, India, Mali, Senegal, Serbia and Montenegro, Sri Lanka)
Medium or Low	38 countries	8 countries (Albania, Guyana, Lesotho, Moldova, Mongolia, Nicaragua, Niger, Papua New Guinea)

(Left axis label: Bureaucratic Capability)

Note: States with higher bureaucratic capability are those with CPIA-budget scores of 4 and above, or both CPIA-admin and CPIA-budget scores of 3.5 and above. States with higher quality of checks-and-balances institutions are those which score "high" on at least two checks-and-balances measures in tables 3.1, 3.3, and 3.6.

Why might patterns such as those in table 3.8 be observed? Figure 3.4 illustrates three possible trajectories for governance turnarounds. These might vary depending on both the initial political impetus within a country, and the longer-term historical processes that can shape and constrain political and institutional reform.

In trajectory 1, a developmentally oriented political leader takes power in a hitherto clientelistic setting (as when President Rawlings took power in Ghana in the early 1980s, or President Museveni in Uganda in the mid-1980s). A common early focus of reform might be to liberalize the economy and strengthen the performance of the public sector. This can emphasize strengthening the capabilities of the public bureaucracy—public administration and financial management, and the service provision front line. The strengthening of checks-and-balances institutions can initially be a low priority, though countries vary as to whether there is an initial weakening of checks and balances relative to the status quo (as in Ghana) or a modest improvement (as in Uganda). But once the reform process matures, the priority for government reform might usefully shift from strengthening bureaucratic authority to enhancing stability by increasing transparency, participation, and accountability of the state. This subsequent phase is, in practice, advanced in Ghana and more tentative in Uganda.

In trajectory 2, a turnaround is initiated by a move to political pluralism. Examples in Africa include democratic transitions over the past 15 years in countries as varied as Benin, Kenya, Malawi, Nigeria, and Zambia. Examples in Eastern Europe include Albania and Romania in the early 1990s. The initial political opening is only a first move in the direction of stronger checks-and-balances institutions. The dotted line signals a second phase of governance reform in which the momentum for greater accountability continues—and the reinvigorated legitimacy that comes from stronger participation and accountability provides a platform for ongoing improvements in bureaucratic capability. Whether and how this subsequent phase unfolds is, of course, an empirical matter.

FIGURE 3.4 Governance Turnarounds—Three Trajectories

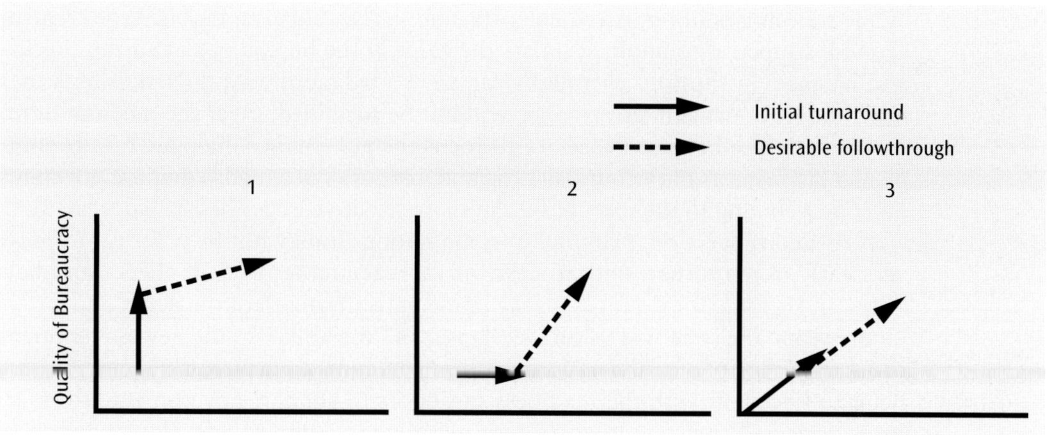

Source: Author.

In trajectory 3, turnaround starts from a state collapse. Sometimes external intervention helps to reintroduce the precondition for an effective state: a monopoly on the legitimate use of violence. This umbrella of security provides an opportunity for reestablishing both the bureaucracy and checks-and-balances institutions. Once a new base has been established, the process can continue in a balanced way, with momentum coming from the newly reestablished domestic institutions. This pattern is evident in countries ranging from Bosnia and Herzegovina to Mozambique.

These varying trajectories pose some dilemmas for the design and sequencing of governance reform:

- Change that focuses first on improvements in bureaucratic quality has the potential for rapid gains in public sector performance. But without a subsequent effort to strengthen checks-and-balances institutions, it risks reversal—perhaps by a reversion to corrupt behavior by the political leadership, perhaps by a loss of legitimacy with citizens.
- Change that begins with a political opening can generate a surge of confidence and improve the climate for private investment. But unless the gains are consolidated, the country risks becoming trapped in a cycle of what Thomas Carothers (Carothers 2002) has called "feckless pluralism"—with short-lived governments repeatedly voted out of power, never having sufficient support and longevity to build the base of bureaucratic capability on which effectiveness and legitimacy will eventually depend.

These varying trajectories also pose dilemmas for a country's development partners—both for scaling up aid (discussed in the conclusion of chapter 2), and for assuring the sustainability of development support.

Sustainability—Bringing Checks and Balances into the Agenda

In the short term, aid can thus straightforwardly be scaled up to countries with improving budget and administrative systems. But a longer-run challenge looms. While trajectories of improvement vary, and in the short run no one type of turn-around is superior to another, unless the gains in the bureaucracy and the checks-and-balances institutions eventually evolve in a balanced way, the risk is high that initial improvements in governance will not be sustained. Over the medium term, it may therefore become necessary to focus the governance dialogue on the complementary aspects of the bureaucratic and institutional agendas that are not spontaneously coming to the fore. How can these sensitive issues best be addressed?

A first consideration is timing. In some settings it may not be practical to press very early in the turnaround process for far-reaching reforms of checks and balances. In Uganda, for example, in the immediate aftermath of the Amin and latter-Obote years, the state was in total collapse, and the ability of the new government to assert authority over the nation was limited. Under such circumstances, it is difficult to find fault with the readiness of donors to support government efforts to focus principally on strengthening bureaucratic capability and development policy, and to emphasize decentralization as a means of bringing government closer to the people. As is well known, far-reaching reductions in Ugandan poverty resulted from the early actions of government and donor support. At the same time, it also seems clear that development partners can wait for too long—until it is too late to put the challenge of strengthening checks and balances squarely on the agenda. An example here is President Suharto's Indonesia—where a failure to focus early enough on checks and balances was associated with rising corruption, financial crisis, and a difficult process of political succession that led to some significant reversal of the development gains of earlier decades. Overall, the track record of recent decades suggests that (perhaps partly as a consequence of the Cold War) in many countries, development partners may have waited too long before putting checks-and-balances institutions higher on the agenda of development dialogue.

A second consideration is that our knowledge of how to get "from here to there" is less developed than our understanding of what well-functioning checks-and-balances institutions should look like. One exception to this proposition is the value of transparency, which is essential for the effective working of all checks and balances, and which can and should be enhanced in almost all settings—at quite low cost. Donors and international financial institutions can play a direct role here, including by ensuring that all analytical work is made widely available, with translation into local languages. We know less as to when and how improvements in transparency translate into genuine gains in accountability and performance, but it does seem to be at least a necessary condition.

Given the limitations of current knowledge, perhaps all that can be offered at this stage is a modest process suggestion. Even—or perhaps especially—when it is still uncomfortable, governments and their development partners might usefully begin a dialogue on how to strengthen checks-and-balances institutions. The aim of this dialogue would be to agree on a phased sequence of steps for strengthening these institutions, perhaps placing an emphasis more directly on those relevant to MDG outcomes—transparency, gender, the justice system, and local governance, for example. Recipient countries would be accountable for proceeding with an agreed sequence. In return, they would enjoy more certainty over what is expected by the international community. Donors, in turn, having agreed on a way forward, would be expected not to shift the goalposts after the fact.

Annex 3.1. Strengths and Weaknesses in Checks-and-Balances Institutions

Annex table 3.1 brings together the country results for the aggregate indicators examined in each of the three main sections of this chapter. The table underscores both the very wide variations in performance across countries, and the striking within-country variation in strengths and weaknesses across different checks-and-balances indicators:

- Twenty-one countries are stronger checks-and-balances performers—in the top group for at least two of the three indicators (and, at a minimum, in the middle group for the third indicator).
- Twenty countries are "weak" performers (with weakness defined as scoring in the bottom group for two of the three indicators, and medium in the third).
- Of the remaining 28 countries, only 4 exhibit consistently middling performance across indicators; an uneven mix of strengths and weaknesses across indicators is more common.

As for the within-country variations in checks-and balances scores:

- Among generally middling performers, Bosnia and Herzegovina, Mozambique, and São Tomé and Principe are identified by the indicators as countries where limitations in formal institutional arrangements are compensated for by an open environment for civil society. By contrast, Ethiopia, Mauritania, Lao People's Democratic Republic, Rwanda, and Vietnam appear to rely more exclusively on formal arrangements (even though their performance on these dimensions scores no better than that of the former three countries).
- At the lower end of the spectrum, the Republic of Congo, Guinea-Bissau and the Republic of Yemen parallel Bosnia and Herzegovina, Mozambique, and São Tomé and Principe in the sense that (severe) weakness in formal arrangements are compensated for by more openness.
- Also at the lower end, six generally weak countries emerge as having one set of formal institutions—for four it is "executive constraints" and for two it is the "rule of law"—seemingly capable of restraining arbitrary executive authority, at least to some extent. Note, though, that the combination of moderately strong "executive constraint," but weak "rule of law" and "voice and accountability" may reflect chronic weakness on the part of the executive, more than an environment that offers at least some systematic protection to citizens and firms from predation.

ANNEX TABLE 3.1 Checks-and-Balances Institutions—Patterns of Country Performance, 2004

Country Performance vis-à-vis Three Sets of Checks-and-Balances Institutions

		Voice and Accountability[a]		
		Low	Medium	High
Executive Constraints (Excon) and the Rule of Law (RoL)[b]	High in both		Armenia, Malawi, Sri Lanka	Ghana, Honduras, India, Lesotho, Mali, Madagascar, Senegal
	High RoL, Medium Excon	Bhutan**	Tanzania	
	High Excon, Medium RoL		Bangladesh, Georgia, Indonesia, Kenya, Moldova, Zambia	Albania, Benin, Bolivia, Comoros, Guyana, Mongolia, Nicaragua, Niger, Papua New Guinea, Serbia and Montenegro, Solomon Islands
	Medium in both	Ethiopia, Mauritania, Lao PDR, Rwanda, Vietnam	Burkina Faso, Cambodia, Djibouti, Uganda	Bosnia and Herzegovina,[xx] Mozambique, Sao Tome and Principe[xx]
	Medium in RoL, low in Excon	Eritrea, Pakistan	Azerbaijan, Gambia, Nepal	
	Medium in Excon, low in RoL	Angola, Guinea, Kyrgyz Republic, Tajikistan	Nigeria,[x] Sierra Leone,[x]	
	Low in Both	Burundi,[xx] Central African Republic, Cameroon, Chad, Congo DR,[xx] Côte d'Ivoire,[xx] Haiti,[xx] Sudan, Togo, Uzbekistan, Zimbabwe	Congo Republic, Guinea-Bissau, Yemen	

Source: Author.
Note:
a. The KK "Voice and Accountability" aggregate governance indicator. Low is defined as being in the bottom third, high is defined as being in the top third., medium is the middle third.
b. For executive constraints, high is defined as a score of 5–7 on the Polity IV index, medium a score of 3–4, and low a score of 1–2. Rule of Law is defined as high for countries in the top two quintiles of the KK Rule of Law indicator, and with scores above 3.0 on the Property Rights and Rule-Based Governance CPIA, it is defined as low for countries in the bottom two KK quintiles, and with the CPIA score under 3.0. All other countries are defined as medium on the Rule of Law.
** = low in Excon, x = high in Excon xx = unscored on Excon

Notes

42. See World Bank, Global Monitoring Report 2006, chapter 7, for a detailed review of global checks-and-balances mechanisms.

43. The Polity project (www.cidcm.umd.edu/inscr/polity), run from the University of Maryland, is the world's most widely used data resource for monitoring regime change and studying the effects of regime authority.

44. Marshall and Jaggers 2002, 23–24.

45. Note that though judicial quality is included in the formal definition, it plays only a modest role in scoring the variable. Note also that neither the definition nor the scaling system incorporates a measure of the extent of ongoing, open operation of civil society. Both conceptually and empirically, the "executive constraints" measure is thus indeed capturing a different facet of checks-and-balances institutions than the other measures to be discussed later. Its correlation with the KK Rule of Law measure is 0.40. The correlation with the KK Voice and Accountability variable is 0.77.

46. At the level of aggregation at which the four subindicators in table 8.1 appear, the GPI has 21 subindicators in all. The specific questions in the table are at the next lowest level of disaggregation (where there is a total of 80 sub-subindicators).

47. Carothers, 1999, 186–87.

48. World Development Report 2004, 90.

49. White and Smoke 2005, 7.

50. WDR 2004, 185.

51. The inception of the term "rule of law" reaches to the roots of Western political thought, for instance, in early Greek and Roman political writings, and also appears as a cornerstone in the genesis of various European legal and political systems. See, e.g., Rigo A., and H.J. Gruss. 1991 for an excellent overview of the origins of the rule of law in Greek and Roman thinking, as well as its emergence as a central tenet in the British and French legal orders. For a more extensive discussion, covering both Western and non-Western conceptions and origins of the rule of law, see Hager (2000), 3–20.

52. This list is taken from Rigo, supra at 4, citing L. Fuller, The Morality of Law, 33–44 (ver. ed. 1969). To be clear, however, while there would be little disputing the value of these specific components, there is no settled or exhaustive set of criteria for the rule of law.

53. Kaufmann, Kraay, and Mastruzzi 2005.

54. This checklist is available at: http://www.coe.int/T/E/Legal_Affairs/Legal_co-operation/Operation_of_justice/Efficiency_of_justice/Documents/.

55. Stephenson 2005, 9.

56. Anderson and Gray 2005.

57. USAID/IFIS study on Independence of the Judiciary.

58. Sage and Woolcock 2005.

59. Sen 1999.

60. "Access to information held by the state is a fundamental right of every individual. States have the obligation to guarantee the full exercise of this right." (http://www.cidh.oas.org/Basicos/principles.htm). Freedom of expression is also protected by Article 13.1 of the Inter-American Convention on Human Rights.

61. OAS 2003, 138.

62. This review of the role of freedom of information laws is adapted from Bellver Ana and Daniel Kaufmann. 2005. "Transparenting Transparency," Working Paper, World Bank, Washington, DC.

63. Adserà, Boix, and Payne 2003, 445–90; Besley and Burgess 2002, 1415–51; Strömberg 2004, 189–221.

64. Consideration was given to using three new measures of transparency produced by Kaufmann and a co-author, but it was decided to stick with the better-known and more thoroughly scrutinized "voice and accountability" measure. The correlation between the aggregate voice and aggregate transparency indicators is 0.88. As for the two transparency subindicators, the correlation between "voice and accountability" and "political transparency" is 0.93. The correlation is much lower—0.41—with the measure of "economic and institutional transparency." But the latter measure generates very large standard errors relative to the other KK indicator, raising questions as to the coherence of the underlying concept it is intended to measure. See Bellver and Kaufmann (2005).

65. Kaufmann, Kraay, and Mastruzzi 2005.

Governance Reform at the Front Line— Service Provision and the Investment Climate

In most countries, top-down reforms of bureaucracies and checks-and-balances institutions of the kind discussed in chapters 2 and 3 will take a long time before they help improve the front-line performance of governments. Low-income countries seeking to turn around their performance thus confront a dilemma. Maintaining the momentum of turnaround may depend on achieving major gains in service provision in the short to medium term. But reforming their formal top-down state accountability systems to the point that they can provide the requisite combination of accountability and responsiveness is a task that will bear fruit only over the long run.

In the face of this dilemma, it is natural to complement top-down reforms with approaches that work more directly at the interface between governments on the one hand, and citizens and firms on the other, including:

- *The provision of services* to citizens and firms, including education, health, utilities, transport infrastructure, and the like.
- *Credible commitment* to private investors as to the stability of the rules of the game. This commitment can result from well-functioning checks-and-balances institutions (especially the justice sector). It can also result from the actions, reputation, and time horizon of the executive.
- *Credible regulation* of markets and criminals, and other antisocial behavior. To function well, a regulatory system needs both bureaucratic capability and credibility, and should operate in a way that keeps the transactional burden on citizens and firms to a minimum.

Top-down and front-line approaches often are perceived to be at odds with each other. A contrasting perspective—and a central theme of this chapter—is that their relationship can be mutually reinforcing. Front-line approaches have the potential to help address a weakness of top-down reforms: aside from the long lags before they deliver results (when they work well), top-down initiatives can be undercut because they are not underpinned by a change in the incentives of political and bureaucratic leaders. They are "upstream," without well-defined front-line actors (firms, citizens, civil society organizations, service users, and so forth) to push for results. As this chapter will explore, especially in weaker governance settings, where expectations and top-down pressures for improved performance may be limited, engaging at the front line has the potential to alter this equation, achieving development results quite quickly, while also potentially helping to accelerate the pressure and momentum for deeper top-down reforms.

The discussion is organized around the governance-related aspects of two sets of challenges that are key to achieving development effectiveness via the front-line—getting the priorities right, and getting the accountabilities right. Getting the priorities right is key because the front-line agenda of governments is a broad one—too broad to be addressed comprehensively in countries with limited resources and capacities. Getting the accountabilities right is key to assuring that front-line agencies use the resources allocated to them well. Monitoring front-line performance will be considered as part of accountability. So, unlike the earlier chapters, here the focus is less on monitoring as a tool of comparative governance assessment, and more on how governance-related informational interventions can improve effectiveness at the front line—and perhaps also help provide momentum for broader systemic reforms.

Getting the Priorities Right

For the past few decades, as work on both public expenditure management and on the investment climate exemplifies, comprehensive, cross-cutting approaches have dominated the reform discourse. For public expenditure management, this has entailed strengthening the institutional arrangements for budget formulation. For the investment climate, this has entailed action on a broad front to address the full range of business environment constraints that inhibit productive private investment. More recently, however, the focus in both areas has shifted toward more targeted approaches that aim to identify and act on specific high-return opportunities.

Prioritizing Public Spending

In setting public expenditure priorities, a continuing challenge is to assure that scarce public resources are targeted toward activities with high social returns, and are deployed efficiently. The development returns can be high from reviewing public expenditures to identify those with high potential returns, and ongoing, low-return expenditures that could usefully be reprioritized toward high-return uses.[66] Where this process works well, the fiscal space opened up for new investment or productive current expenditure can be large:

- Chile invested on average 5 percent of GDP in infrastructure during the second half of the 1990s without resorting to significant borrowing, primarily through reallocation of expenditure, increased efficiency, and the use of public-private partnerships. One consequence was that the country's credit rating increased, enlarging its unused borrowing capacity, and giving it greater fiscal flexibility for potential future use.
- Thailand in 2005 initiated a large five-year public investment program of 2.5–5 percent of GDP annually to upgrade and improve infrastructure, addressing widely recognized bottlenecks, including mass transit in Bangkok, and the country's interprovincial highways. Credit rating agencies have assessed the investment program to be an important driver of growth over the medium term—assessments that were based on the country's earlier fiscal credibility, and enabled it to finance these investments via borrowing. However, both the IMF and rating agencies have noted that effective management of the investment program will be needed to ensure continued access to markets.
- The United Kingdom routinely incorporates spending reviews into its budget preparation process. Despite this, a 2003 independent review of public sector efficiency identified over US$15 billion of ongoing spending that was not being efficiently used, and was directly "cash releasing," and so available for reallocation.

One goal of public expenditure management reforms is to put in place systems that routinely review and recalibrate priorities. But for all of the potential benefits of such arrangements, putting them in place is difficult for at least three reasons. First, as chapter 2 has detailed, in many low-income countries even the basics of cross-cutting budget and administrative systems do not work well. Second, even where the systems work well, they might not drill down in sufficient detail to distinguish effectively between low- and high-return activities: the knowledge needed to assess development returns can be highly specialized, and reside within sectors, not in central budget agencies. Third, many high-return investments cut across sectoral boundaries, as illustrated by the high benefits for childhood health that come from upgrading wood-burning stoves or dirt floors.

While the returns are high from strengthening budget systems so they can prioritize more effectively, especially in low-income and weaker governance settings, the need to use resources well is too urgent to be dependent solely on systemic improvements. The case is compelling for complementing efforts at improvements in the system with more targeted efforts—within individual sectors and across sectors—to identify high-return investment opportunities, plus opportunities for freeing up resources locked into low-return activities. This is an activity for which development partners can provide targeted assistance. The Public Expenditure Reviews facilitated by the World Bank, already an established part of the landscape of development dialogue, offer a ready-made vehicle.

Prioritizing Investment Climate Reforms

It is broadly accepted that a good investment climate is key to private sector-led growth. As the 2005 World Development Report, *A Better Investment Climate for Everyone,* detailed, the components of a good investment climate are many and varied, including macro stability, property rights, reduced crime, business regulation, tax and trade policy, financial markets, infrastructure, workforce quality, industrial policy, and labor market regulation. A common response to this breadth has been "to reform as much as possible, to pursue whatever reforms seem practical and politically feasible…implicitly relying on the notion that any reform is good; the more areas reformed, the better, and the deeper the reform in any area the better."[67] Especially in settings where capacity and political will is weak, the likelihood is low that such an approach will ease the most binding constraints to growth. In response, new approaches to investment climate reform aim to directly target these binding constraints. This section will describe these approaches, highlighting their governance dimensions.

The conceptual framework. Figure 4.1 depicts a decision tree, which helps identify the biggest obstacles to growth. The decision tree distinguishes among three seemingly mutually exclusive causes of low growth—the high cost of finance, low social returns to economic activity, and low appropriability by private actors of social returns. Ten specific constraints to growth underlie the three broad causes. Which of these constraints is likely to be binding will vary across countries and over time. The aim of investment climate reform is to identify and alleviate the key constraints.

Note that many of the specific constraints to growth need governance reforms to be addressed effectively:

- Easing constraints linked to low social returns—bad infrastructure, low human capital—needs better bureaucratic capability. Bureaucratic capability also affects the quality of monetary, fiscal, and financial market policies and regulation.
- Easing constraints linked to government failures and associated weaknesses in credible commitment—the protection of property rights, control of corruption—needs better checks-and-balances institutions.
- Easing constraints linked to market failures needs proactive, market-enhancing government interventions. To be effective, market-enhancing interventions generally require a capable state—both high levels of bureaucratic capability and skillful use of discretionary authority by implementing agencies, with the latter implying the presence of checks and balances capable of restraining arbitrary, counterproductive discretion.

Note also that the approach implies that governance reform might often more usefully be sector specific—targeting the most binding constraints—rather than focused on cross-cutting, upstream systems. As amplified later in this section, an approach to governance reform that targets specific binding constraints to growth can be very different from the approach described in chapters 2 and 3. The approach in these chapters was top-down—identifying and reforming broad, cross-cutting dysfunctions in governance institutions. By contrast, the binding constraints approach aims to narrowly identify and target very specific interventions, with the aim of getting very specific results in the short and medium term.

Sometimes, to be sure, the seeming specificity is illusory. For example, government failures tied to weak checks and balances and an inability to make credible commitments can be rooted in deep dysfunctions in political institutions, which

FIGURE 4.1   Obstacles to Growth

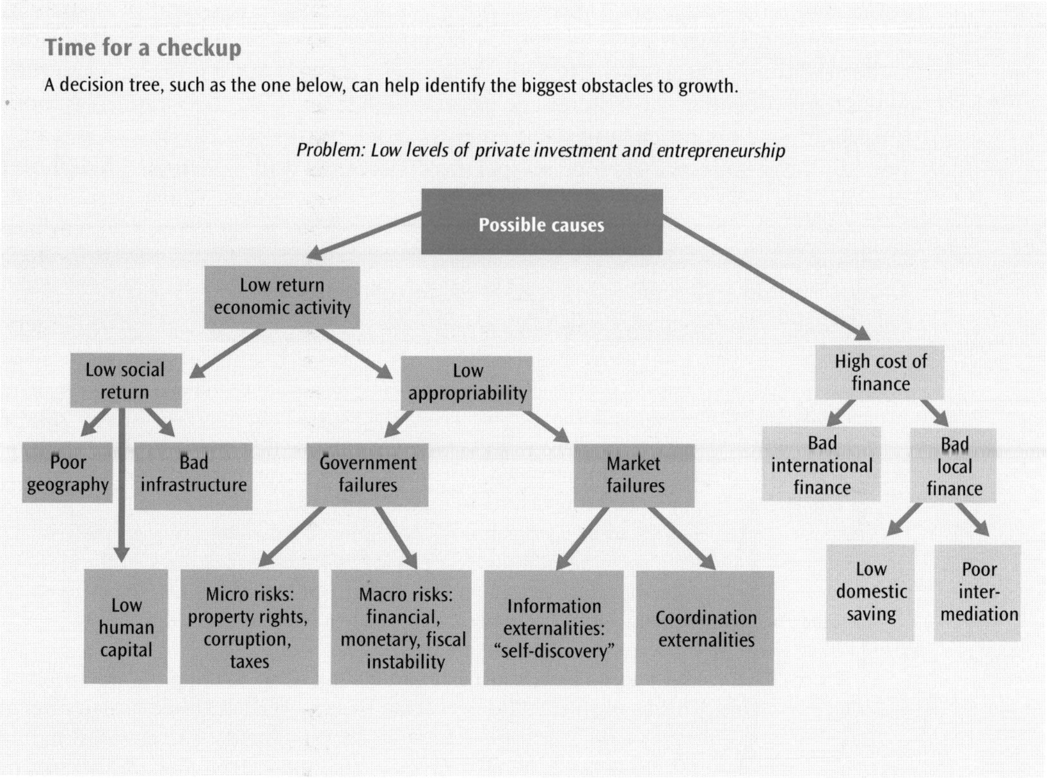

Time for a checkup

A decision tree, such as the one below, can help identify the biggest obstacles to growth.

Problem: Low levels of private investment and entrepreneurship

Source: Hausmann, Rodrik, and Velasco 2006.

undermine the quality of political competition (see box 1.3 in chapter 1), shorten the time horizon of politicians, and more broadly undercut state legitimacy. Similarly, as noted above, only a broadly capable state is likely to be able to leverage the informational and coordination externalities needed to overcome a seeming dearth of evident opportunities for profitable investment. In other settings, though, the binding constraints approach will indeed point to specific constraints that can be addressed through targeted actions—often agency specific and bottom up. As box 4.1 illustrates with the example of power sector reform in Andhra Pradesh, India, the politics of reform often imply that the actions needed to alleviate the specific constraint may not be those that seem "first best."

Identifying the constraints. Comparative country surveying and benchmarking seem a natural way to identify country-specific constraints to growth. Indeed, both the DB and ICS surveys described in chapter 2 are potentially powerful tools for constraints analysis.

Figure 4.2 (taken from the 2005 WDR, 59) highlights nine different areas that are reported by firms to be the top constraint in at least 1 of 49 countries where ICS data are available. Policy uncertainty and macro instability emerged as the top constraints in 50 percent of the countries; taxes, regulation, and corruption in an additional 34 percent; and infrastructure, finance, skills, crime, and the courts in the remaining 16 percent.

But the implications of the ICS and DB results may be more nuanced than they first seem. Consider the differences between what entrepreneurs report as their most binding constraints, and what emerges from a statistical analysis of the relationship between the incidence of specific constraints and enterprise growth. As

---

BOX 4.1   The Politics of Electricity Reform in Andhra Pradesh, India

In 1997, Andhra Pradesh's power sector absorbed subsidies amounting to 1.6 percent of state GDP, an amount greater than the annual cost of providing primary health care and clean drinking water to rural villages throughout the state. Behind these costs lay a complex interaction between nontransparent operation of the sector and local politics.

The lack of transparency was tied to an untouchable political commitment to provide free power to agricultural consumers. Free power translated into unmetered power, and provided a seeming rationale for the fact that only 42 percent of the electricity flowing into the distribution system was actually billed on the basis of metered consumption. But this rationale was not credible: disaggregated surveys pointed to endemic consumer dissatisfaction and corruption in the sector.

Power sector employees and consumers were colluding in making unmonitored power available (for side payments) to users who, by law, were supposed to pay.

In 1998, a reformist state government decided to tackle the problem head on. It put in place specific legal and organizational measures to enforce greater accountability in the sector. And it complemented these with a series of actions anchored in a clear understanding of the political dynamics, and a clear recognition of how coalition building and a push for transparency could counter the dysfunctional dynamics.

A major communications campaign was launched, signaling a commitment to the goals of improving customer service and reducing connection delays—and signaling also that strict new penalties would be enforced for electricity theft. At the same time, town hall meetings throughout the state provided the opportunity for on-the-spot authorization (after paying a connection fee) of preexisting illegal connections. Better metering of consumption was key; more than 2 million high-quality meters were installed in two years (compared with an earlier annual average of 600,000). While agricultural customers remained unmetered, meters were installed on the transformers serving mainly these customers to allow better estimates of service to agriculture. The commitment to stop hiding behind the excuse that free power to agriculture accounted for the seeming system losses led by 1999 to an upward revision of transmission and distribution "losses" aside from agriculture (principally through rampant electricity theft) from 18 percent to 38 percent.

By 2003, the stringent theft controls had begun to bite. Transmission and distribution losses fell by one-third from four years earlier, to 26 percent. And, over the same period, revenue collected by the system rose by 50 percent.

Source: Bhatia and Gulati 2004, and related Powerpoint presentation.

---

table 4.1 summarizes, the statistical exercise yields a common set of top three binding constraints for Bangladesh, Nigeria, and Singapore—financing, street crime, and political instability (all statistically significant). In all three countries, though, the perceived constraints are quite different from these, and different from one country to another.

As a second illustration, consider the distinction between the de jure and de facto burdens of doing business.[68] Table 4.2 uses many of the DB and ICS variables highlighted in annex table 1.2. The first rows report the 2005 DB rankings of the quality of

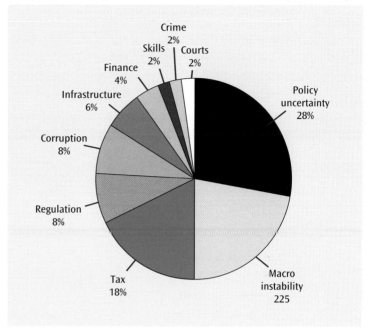

FIGURE 4.2 The Top Investment Climate Concern of Firms (49 countries)

Source: World Development Report (2005b), derived from World Bank Investment Climate Surveys in 49 countries, based on rankings by country.

the de jure rules for four governance-related measures for Bangladesh, Kenya, and Tanzania. All three countries score poorly, with Kenya rating perhaps a little better than the others. But the realities on the ground in the three countries, evident from the results of the ICS surveys, do not correspond to these de jure patterns.

As the table shows, Tanzania's de jure rigidities indeed signal a rigid business environment. The ICS results show that senior management of firms spend over 14 percent of their time dealing with regulations. Dealing with tax officials and clearing exports or imports through customs each take 10 or more days. In contrast, Bangladesh's business environment is lubricated by corruption: all three measures in the table show corruption to be substantially worse in Bangladesh than Tanzania. But the data also reveal what businesses in Bangladesh buy for their corruption—much less hassle in practice in dealing with government officials. Corruption also is rife in Kenya—consistently higher than in Tanzania, and higher than in Bangladesh for two of the three measures. Unlike in Bangladesh, though, with senior management spending close to 12 percent of their time dealing with regulations, the lubricating impact of Kenya's corruption seems limited.

To be sure, neither a lubricated nor a rigid business environment is as good for growth as an environment that is transactionally efficient. But equally sure, the impediments of the de jure burdens as a constraint on growth would appear to be greater for Tanzania—and in a different way for Kenya—than for Bangladesh. However, as Bangladesh, which is currently growing rapidly, moves

TABLE 4.1   Top 3 Constraints to Enterprise Investment—Perceived and Computed

	Estimated impact on firm growth[a]	Top three perceived constraints		
		Bangladesh	Nigeria	Singapore
Financing	1			1
Street crime	2			
Political instability	3	3	2	
Corruption		1	3	
Exchange rate		2		2
Infrastructure			1	
Inflation				3

Source: Ayyagari, Demirguc-Kunt and Maksimovic 2005.
Note: a. The ranking of estimated impact was the same for all three countries.

up the value chain, the constraints imposed on growth by corruption are likely to become more severe.

As the above attests, the interrelations among constraints to private sector-led growth can be quite subtle. DB and ICS surveys offer valuable information in helping to identify binding constraints. But the challenge of prioritizing reform of the investment climate cannot be reduced to some mechanical, data-driven formula.

Following through on Prioritization: Enclaves and Their Discontents

Once binding constraints on growth and priority areas for public spending are identified, a natural followup is to prioritize implementation along the same, focused lines. But the challenges can be formidable to integrating focused, front-line approaches to implementation on the one hand, and more systemic reform goals on the other.

One common approach has been to create a self-standing investment project, complete with its own project implementation unit; however, as box 4.2 describes, such parallel approaches can exacerbate the difficulties of improving governance more broadly. A second response has been to focus much more narrowly on improving performance in those specific subparts of the public sector that are both priority areas for reform and have some room for maneuver. As the examples of community schools, road funds, and export zones illustrate, sometimes reforms proceed via sector-specific changes in rules and institutions, which result in some "enclaving" from the rest of the public sector.

Sector-specific reforms—community schools and road funds. Focusing reform sectorally has the potential to achieve many goals simultaneously:

- achieving some quick wins in a high-priority area
- in weaker governance settings, providing a mechanism for using the limited country capacity for policy formulation and implementation in a focused way

TABLE 4.2   Transactions Costs of Doing Business—DB and ICS Results

	Kenya	Bangladesh	Tanzania
De jure rules (DB country rank)			
Starting a business	93	52	113
Dealing with licenses	15	53	150
Registering property	113	151	143
Trading across borders	126	125	102
Corruption (ICS)			
Bribes/Sales (%)	2.9%	2.1%	1.3%
Gifts in meetings with tax officials (% firms)	37.0%	86.0%	22.4%
Gift value (% government contract)	6.5%	4.0%	2.9%
De facto burden (ICS)			
Senior management time dealing with regulations (%)	11.7%	3.7%	14.4%
Time spent with tax officials (days)	4	2	12
Average time to clear exports through customs (days)	4	8	10
Average time to claim imports from customs (days)	8	10	15

Sources: www.doingbusiness.org; www.enterprisesurveys.org

■ providing a clear focal point for results-based monitoring and evaluation, thereby helping assure mutual accountability on the part of both donors and the recipient government and ministry

The push worldwide for road funds, and the move toward community schools and contracting of teachers, illustrate both the potential benefits—and the potential complications—for subsequent systemic reforms. Consider first the benefits:

■ Governance of road funds often is part of a broader effort to create a partnership between road users and government. This crowds into oversight users who have a stake in the efficient and honest use of resources (including stakeholders from the road transport industry, chambers of commerce, farmers' organizations, and professional institutions). In addition to their interest in decent roads, users also have an incentive to provide oversight because, in the road fund model, some of the revenues used for road investment and maintenance come from (at least notionally) earmarked vehicle licenses and fuel levies.[69]

■ Sectorwide programs in education sometimes (notably in francophone Africa) have included a move toward community schools, with increased parental oversight. Such oversight has been shown to improve both school management and educational outcomes.[70] In addition, locating at least some responsibility for the contracting of teachers with communities, with contracting terms reflecting local conditions, helps resources go further. As the 2005 Global Monitoring Report put it: "Skilled providers are the biggest expense in any social sector budget, as well as the most essential input for effective service delivery...new recruitment

> **BOX 4.2 Why Stand-Alone Investment Projects Can Be Bad for Governance**
>
> Over the past half-century, stand-alone investment projects have been the dominant response of external donors to the dilemma of ensuring accountability in weaker-governance settings. Projects implemented by autonomous units have a useful role, especially for large infrastructure initiatives. But from a governance perspective, the turn to wholly parallel, projectized arrangements is a conclusion of despair. Such projects substitute external for local accountabilities, thereby perpetuating weaknesses in national governance systems. They typically insulate themselves from the day-to-day business (and rules) of the public sectors in the countries in which they operate: they establish independent project implementation units; set up their own procedures; offer salaries higher than those available in the civil service; and attract away the best talent, demoralizing those who remain. Reducing the prevalence of separate project implementation units is therefore a high priority of many donors.

strategies lower costs per beneficiary served...even when offering average salaries as low as half the civil service teacher wage, countries have found more qualified applicants than they can hire..."[71]

Despite their advantages, such sectorally focused initiatives can be at variance with standard approaches to strengthening cross-cutting bureaucratic controls:

- Ring-fencing through road funds can undercut the ability to make choices between competing uses of resources, fragment the systems of budgetary control, and complicate efforts to achieve broader improvements in the financial management system.
- Community contracting of teachers risks undercutting efforts to introduce transparent and meritocratic practices of recruitment and promotion, and can also create new opportunities for informality and patronage.

Each of these criticisms presumes that broader systemic reforms are directly feasible. But in most early turnaround situations this is unlikely to be the case: The challenge is to achieve gains in an imperfect world, where the best can be the enemy of the good. Further, partial reforms also have the potential to nudge along incremental change in broader systems: A well-managed road fund can help achieve stable financing within the sector and establish well-functioning financial management controls—and thereby be a spur to more far-reaching systemic public financial management reforms. A move toward community teachers might create an opening for reform towards more pluralistic—though no less transparent or meritocratic—approaches to civil service reform. And engaging citizens in the task of public sector governance within individual sectors can be a valuable spur to civic engagement more broadly.

Promoting exports. A common approach to improving the investment climate, one consistent with the binding constraints approach outlined earlier, is to identify and support sectors (including the export sector) with high growth potential. This approach has long been confronted with skepticism, both for fear that a narrow focus on exports will short-circuit systemic reform, and for a more specific private sector-related reason: the risk seemed high that targeted interventions by public actors would translate into "picking winners," counterproductively superseding the market. Despite this skepticism, the combination of difficulties in implementing the broad agenda, and the possibility of "quick wins" have led to a renewed interest in more focused approaches.

EPZs are a common example of this type of narrow approach.[72] By the end of 2002, some 3,000 EPZs had been created in 116 countries, providing jobs for some 43 million workers—most of them women. In some countries, they have played a central role in kick-starting growth:

- In 1989, China designated four Special Economic Zones, in nearby Hong Kong, China, and Taiwan, China—three in Guandong province and one in the Fukian province. The zones offered special incentives to foreign investors. Infrastructure and the legal framework for FDI were also improved. The average annual growth rate in the Shenzen zone alone exceeded 35 percent in 1980–95. The zones soon expanded to other areas, with a progressive opening of more coastal areas to foreign investment in the 1980s, and increased opening of inland provinces in the 1990s.
- Mauritius used EPZs as part of a successful strategy to spur export-led growth and diversify its economy. It did it with a twist—EPZ status was granted to wholly export-oriented firms, independent of location. Manufactured exports grew at 5.9 percent a year between 1991 and 2001, and accounted for 73 percent of merchandise exports in 2002. Employment in the EPZs ranges between 80,000 and 90,000. Many workers in the foreign sector later created their own businesses.
- In the Dominican Republic, tourism and the maquila sector (the assembly of imported parts for reexport) were the main drivers of growth. Like the rest of the economy, they faced problems relating to infrastructure, security, and trade protectionism. But rather than tackle these difficult problems across the economy, the government insulated these two sectors and provided targeted solutions, improving security and infrastructure around the main tourist areas and giving the maquila sector special trade policy treatment.

The impact of a successful export push on the momentum for continuing improvement of the investment climate is mixed. On the one hand, exporters can quickly become a powerful lobby for strengthening the public sector (infrastructure and regulatory-related transactions costs) parts of the value chain that are critical to their market success. On the other hand, targeted approaches to promote exports confront a challenge of assuring that they link to the broader economy, and do not end up as dead-end islands of effectiveness amid a nonreforming sea of continuing private sector backwardness. China overcame this quite rapidly: while initially most inputs used in the Special Economic Zones were imported, local content grew over the 1990s. Many countries establish special programs designed to foster spillovers from foreign direct investment, with the "linkage" programs of Singapore and Ireland notably successful.

Getting the Accountabilities Right

To perform effectively, front-line providers need the right balance of flexibility and accountability for results. As the 2004 World Development Report *Making Services Work for Poor People* highlighted, getting this balance right can be challenging, and the challenges are different in strong and weak governance settings. This section will consider the challenge of improving accountability at the front line from two perspectives.

The first perspective focuses on accountability from the top down. A universal challenge is to assert control without straitjacketing front-line agencies with excessively rigid rules. Getting the balance right between flexibility and control has been a key theme of efforts at public management reform in many OECD countries—from New Zealand's pioneering experiments, to the American Reinventing Government initiative, to myriad other experiments under the New Public Management (NPM) label. It has also been a central preoccupation of efforts to assure efficient private participation and regulation in infrastructure utilities. Note, though, that the legacy in many low-income settings is not so much excess control as it is excess informality—weak controls, arbitrary discretion at all levels of the bureaucracy, and corruption.

The second perspective focuses on bottom-up accountability. The aim here is to try and get results at the front line by complementing top-down efforts with more participatory apporaches to accountability. In all countries, bottom-up accountabilities (that is, provider accountability to users, communities, firms, and citizens) can be an important complement to more top-down approaches. In addition, in settings where top-down accountability is weak, bottom-up accountabilities may be a useful short-run mechanism for assuring that resources that find their way to the public service front line are well used. But, as with the earlier discussion of enclaves, such approaches also risk making it more difficult to build institutions capable of sustaining efforts at poverty reduction over the long run. The second subsection will examine the role of bottom-up accountabilities to citizens and firms—both as an integral part of the accountability system in all countries, and as an approach that may hold unusual potential in weaker governance settings, but also bring unusual challenges.

Top-Down Accountability—Balancing Flexibility and Control

Finding the right balance between flexibility and control is a ubiquitous challenge in the design of institutions. As two diverse examples—new public management, and private participation and regulation in infrastructure utilities—illustrate, the dilemma is especially acute in countries where governance is weaker, and so lack the checks-and-balances institutions that make it possible to underpin flexibility with accountability for pursuing the public interest.

The new public management. The past two decades have seen a worldwide mushrooming of reform efforts in high- and middle-income countries aimed at strengthening the results orientation of public service providers. Worldwide, the intent of reforms is to shift the focus of top-down state control from inputs to outputs. Policy makers are to define clearly *what* should be done, and to set performance targets as a basis for monitoring the performance of front-line providers. Against the backdrop of clarity with respect to goals and accountability for results, front-line providers are to be given the flexibility to decide *how* things are to be done.

NPM was designed for, and works best in, countries with well-developed bureaucracies. Where such countries have worked to shift toward a more results-oriented approach to public management, they generally have introduced four sets of interdependent changes.

- First is reorienting input controls. Traditional bureaucracies have long been governed via tight ex ante centralized controls over inputs of the kind examined in chapter 2. The NPM approach to input control aims to reduce rigidities on front-line providers, but in a framework that ensures effectiveness and probity in how the resources are used.
- Second is clarifying the performance framework within which front-line providers are to operate. For public providers, this framework could take the form of agreed upon upfront targets of performance. For private providers, the framework could comprise the regulatory rules of the game that set the constraints within which profit-seeking activity might proceed.
- Third is strengthening the mechanisms for holding providers accountable as to whether agreed-upon results were achieved. Some of these mechanisms are internal to the administrative system (for example, linking budgets with performance, or linking staff promotion to performance); others take the form of strengthening transparency and accountability of public actors vis-à-vis civil society (by, for example, providing service delivery performance indicators to users, or by involving users and other citizens at local levels more directly in governance and oversight).
- Fourth, strengthening monitoring and evaluation systems to provide an empirical basis for assessing results (outputs—whether resources achieved their intended proximate objectives; and outcomes—whether the social purpose for which the resources were deployed was achieved), and thereby providing a basis (other than compliance with input controls) for holding public agencies accountable for how effectively they have used public resources.

Note that, though the focus of control shifts from inputs to outputs, all four changes leave intact the underlying commitment to formal, top-down state accountability.

The Executive Agency model, introduced in the United Kingdom in 1988, is an example of results-oriented public management reform and what it can achieve.[73] EAs are separate business units, with well-defined outputs. In return for budget resources, agencies commit themselves to performance targets and report on these targets in an annual report. Employees remain public officers, and agencies normally have no separate corporate status—in other words, they and their staffs remain part of government. Some agencies, though, have been given the freedom to recruit staff on terms and conditions more favorable than the civil service and closer to private sector levels for key technical, professional, and managerial staff. Within a decade of the program's inauguration, 150 agencies had been established. Since 1988, the civil service has been reduced from 570,000 to fewer than 480,000, while performance and functions have increased. Staff in EA and other executive organizations presently account for 373,000 or 78 percent, of the central civil service. The keys to success are a clearly defined mandate and outputs, and an effective accountability framework and result-oriented performance management, documented by regular annual reports. Critically, the United Kingdom adopted the EA model from the starting point of an ethical, motivated, and well-paid civil service that operates in accordance with the formal rules. But the positive British experience is hardly the norm among reforming countries. The review cited in chapter 2 of experience with public administrative reform in 10 OECD countries found that:

> To launch, sustain and implement a comprehensive strategy for reform requires certain conditions...a high degree of consensus over what needs to be done, sustained over five-years-plus...informed leadership, both from politicians and top public civil servants...considerable organizational capacity...and a degree of public acceptance. These are seldom all satisfied in the real world of public management reform. Occasionally the list of requirements may be more or less met—in New Zealand between 1984 and 1990 for example...Often, however, one or more important requirements cannot be satisfied. Even in the most favorable circumstances, conditions may change. Or the implementation capacity is insufficient, and well meant reforms get bogged down.[74]

The interest in NPM in high-income countries has inspired similar efforts in middle-income countries (Turkey and Thailand, for example) and even some low-income ones (Tanzania). Unsurprisingly, in even the better-governed developing countries, the track record of moving to this type of results-oriented approach is mixed. Consider the experience of Thailand, which embarked on reforms to enhance the flexibility and accountability of front-line providers as an outgrowth of the 1997 Asian financial crisis, a resulting commitment to reduce aggregate government spending, and a corresponding desire to get more value for money out of public spending.[75]

The Thais confronted a difficult dilemma. On the one hand, the evidence was compelling that the prevailing system of centralized control (notably of the budget) was a key cause of the ineffectiveness of the country's public agencies: Thailand has a long legacy of highly centralized budget control, with agency spending patterns set at the center, and detailed line-item control over budget execution (all by the Bureau of the Budget). The predictable result was that, with no responsibility for how funds were spent, public agencies had only limited incentive or opportunity to attend to performance. On the other hand, strong line-item budgeting comprised Thailand's longstanding and effective mechanism of maintaining fiscal control. Thus, when in 1997 Thailand's political leadership decided to move to performance management, it opted to experiment with an innovative incremental strategy for transforming the relationship between control and accountability—a "hurdle" approach:

- Agencies were invited to move voluntarily to performance management, by clarifying their visions, objectives, strategies, and measurable outputs to achieve these goals.

- Benchmarks were set as to the requisite financial control capabilities at agency level, and the Bureau of the Budget agreed to relinquish detailed central controls of individual agencies as and when they met these benchmarks.
- Participation was intended to be demand driven, with the intent that the pioneers in performance management be those agencies that were most committed to the experiment, and thus most willing to invest in the requisite control systems. [Six pilot agencies were identified upfront, to initiate the process.]

Yet for all of its seemingly attractive features, the "hurdle" experiment failed. The proximate reason was that the benchmarks initially were set at too demanding a level. The more fundamental reason for failure was the reluctance of the Bureau of the Budget and other control agencies to embrace reform. An adviser to the reform process explained this reluctance as follows:

> *Achieving reform in public sector administration should be seen as a political rather than an administrative problem. It is difficult for a budget office to itself reform a highly centralized budget system. There are too many bureaucratic stakeholders who are adversely affected by reform, too much lethargy, and too little leadership in an environment of superintendence rather than management. The benefits of reform do not accrue to officials required to lead the reform effort. Many incur costs—loss of power or other benefits.*[76]

Even in better-governed countries, the move toward a more flexible, results-oriented approach to service provision remains a work in progress.

Private participation and regulation in infrastructure utilities. Complementing NPM, another innovation aimed at improving service provision was the move to private ownership of front-line utility providers. In many developing countries, this move, too, is a work in progress. As with NPM, the vision, summarized in a 2004 World Bank Policy Research Report, Regulating Infrastructure, was clear:

> *In many developing and transition economies state-owned infrastructure monopolies suffered from low labor productivity, deteriorating fixed facilities and equipment, and serious problems of theft and nonpayment...Privatization was heralded as an elixir that would rejuvenate lethargic, wasteful infrastructure industries and revitalize stagnating economies....Network utilities should be unbundled, with potentially competitive segments under separate ownership from natural monopoly components....segments where natural monopoly conditions persist and are unavoidable should be regulated.*[77]

Since the late 1980s, thousands of concession contracts have been awarded around the world. In 1997, annual investment in private infrastructure projects peaked at $130 billion. But subsequently, the process stalled. By 2001, private infrastructure investments had fallen to less than half their 1997 levels. Paralleling the difficulties of implementing NPM, one key reason for this decline was the difficulty, in institutionally weaker country settings of finding the right balance between flexibility and control.[78]

With private utilities, the tension between flexibility and control arises because of three competing pressures. The first pressure is to provide private providers with credible commitments as to the stability of the rules of the game necessary to support large, irreversible infrastructure investments. A natural way to do this is to build very precise terms into the concession contracts signed with private investors. But, as the example in box 4.3 of Chilean electricity in the late 1990s attests, the resulting rigidities conflict with the second pressure—to be able to adapt flexibly to emerging problems, changing circumstances, and new information and experiences.

In principle, regulatory institutions offer a natural resolution to the tension; a credible regulatory regime can handle adjustments without placing strain on the contractual relationship. But, to be credible, regulators must not become politi-

---

BOX 4.3 Regulatory Imbalances in Chile and Jamaica— Some History

Chile. In 1981–82, Chile introduced a new electricity law to assure potential investors that the regulator would not expropriate their investments. The power to make decisions was taken away from the regulator and embedded in the law, which made it comprehensive and complex. At the time this seemed like a good approach: in the early 1980s Chile needed to convince investors that the rules of the game would not change based on regulatory whim. This system attracted investment. But the system's inflexibility became quite costly during the 1998–9 drought. During the crisis, the entire regulatory system collapsed, and the country suffered prolonged blackouts, causing US$300 million in damage to the economy. The failure of regulation during the crisis was partly due to the lack of flexibility embedded in the law, which limited the regulator's ability to respond quickly to the drought.

Jamaica. During much of the colonial period and in the years immediately following independence, the terms under which Jamaica's largest telecommunication utility operated were laid out in a legally binding, precisely specified, 40-year license contract. Then, as now, the ultimate court of appeal for Jamaica's independent judiciary was the Privy Council in the United Kingdom. This system was adequate to ensure steady growth: The number of subscribers tripled between 1950 and 1962. Yet a newly independent Jamaica chafed under the apparent restrictiveness of a concession arrangement that afforded virtually no opportunity for democratic participation. Consequently, in 1966 the country established the Jamaican Public Utility Commission. Modeled on the U.S. system, the commission held regular public hearings and was afforded broad scope to base its regulatory decisions on inputs from a wide variety of stakeholders. But there were virtually no checks and balances on commission decisions. The result was that price controls became progressively more punitive, to the point that in 1975, Jamaica's largest private telecommunications operator was relieved to sell its assets to the government. [The system was reprivatized in 1987, under arrangements which assured rapid increases in investment.]

Sources: Kessides 2004, 110, and World Bank, *World Development Report 1997*, box 4.4, 70.

cized, capricious, corrupt, grossly inefficient, or captured by the utilities they are supposed to regulate. The example in box 4.3 of Jamaican telecommunications regulation in the 1960s illustrates how flexibility can turn sour.

In theory, the right regulatory balance between flexibility and control can be achieved by writing statutes that specify the rights and responsibilities of the regulatory agency; putting in place administrative procedures that foster transparency in the way regulators go about their business; subjecting agency decisions to review by courts; fostering transparency; and subjecting the performance of regulators to formal review by independent auditors or legislative committees. But to work effectively, these restraints need a broader environment of reasonably well-functioning checks-and-balances institutions. Where this broader governance environment is weak, the third pressure—the risk of opportunistic behavior by private firms, regulators, or politicians, comes into play.

Excluding telecommunications, more than 40 percent of concession contracts awarded since the late 1980s have been renegotiated, and 60 percent of these were renegotiated within their first three years, despite contract periods of 15 to 20 years. More than 80 percent of contracts in the water and transportation sectors were renegotiated. As the 2004 World Bank infrastructure study notes: "because rejecting a request from an operator to renegotiate soon after a concession has been awarded may result in its abandonment or suspension—with large political costs for the government that embarked on the process—renegotiation often favors operators…a bidder who knows that early renegotiation is possible may submit an unrealistically low bid with a view to renegotiating better terms (without competition) shortly after securing the concession contract…The preponderance of renegotiation strongly suggests opportunistic behavior and flawed contract design."[79] The contrast between the exuberant enthusiasm for private infrastructure in the mid-1990s, and the more sober assessment a decade later is striking:

> *The fact that state ownership is flawed does not mean that privatization is appropriate for all infrastructure activities and all countries. Before state ownership is supplanted by another institutional setup, it is essential to assess the properties and requirements of the proposed alternative—taking into account [both] the sector's features, and the country's economic, institutional, social and political characteristics… (8)…Among the most critical tasks for policymakers in developing and transition countries is designing and implementing stable, effective regulation for utilities that provide a credible commitment to safeguarding the interests of both investors and customers… (17)…Political interference has undermined regulatory independence in many developing and transition economies…the experience so far raises doubts that governments will observe the spirit of the law and implement proper, consistent regulatory procedures.[80] (18)*

Bottom-Up Accountability—Empowering Front Line Clients

The second perspective from which this section examines how to strengthen accountability comprises improvement at the service provision front line. In all countries, strengthening the accountability of front-line agencies to users (citizens, communities, and firms) can be a useful complement to more top-down approaches to accountability. The impact can be more profound, though, in governance settings where top-down systems and accountabilities are weak. As the two approaches described in this subsection will illustrate, in such settings the skillful use of bottom-up empowerment can make a huge difference in the quality of service provision. The first approach uses citizen engagement in the collection and dissemination of information on service quality and resource use to build demand for better services and more accountability. The second approach engages citizens and communities more directly in service provision.

Using information to improve accountability. Open information on the performance of public agencies can engage citizens in a continuum of ways. At one end is political accountability. Citizens can use information on the quality of service provision as part of their decision to support the reelection of incumbents at national or local levels. At the other end is the use of performance information by citizens directly involved in the governance of service provision facilities, for example through community-driven approaches discussed a little later.

The 2004 World Development Report described vividly a powerful intermediate role for information along this continuum. The WDR argues strongly that to be useful, information on the performance of public agencies must be specific:

> *identifying specific government decisions, specific decision makers, and the effect of the decision on voters individually or as a group... Information about broad aggregates of public sector performance—whether based on surveys, budget studies or other methods—is less likely to be politically relevant. ... At the end of the day, these efforts tell citizens what they already knew—that services are bad...What citizens do not have, and what they need help in getting, is information about how bad their neighborhood's services are relative to others' and who is responsible for the difference.*[81]

A first example of the potential of empowerment through information highlights how detailed, public information can enable citizens to make informed judgments regarding the performance of politicians, policy makers, and providers, and to respond with support, or pressure for change. Frustrated by years of inaction on public services, which increasingly were unable to keep up with Bangalore's dynamism and population pressure, a group of citizens in 1994 introduced the idea of a user survey-based "report card" on public services. Initially, the impact was modest. As the pioneer of the initiative put it:

> *It is unrealistic to expect public agencies to respond immediately and directly to the signals given by a report card. Agency leaders need the time and capacity to internalize the messages of the report card and design interventions to address the issues raised. Civil society institutions also need time and resources to get organized and plan strategies to interact with service providers.*[82]

Nonetheless, the sponsors persisted, establishing an NGO, the Bangalore Public Affairs Center, to institutionalize the effort, building coalitions with other NGOs

FIGURE 4.3 Perceptions of Service Delivery Performance in Nine Bangalore Agencies, 1994–2003

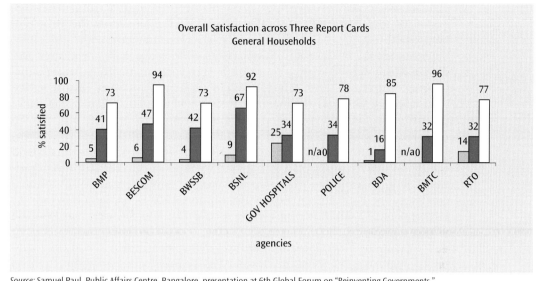

Source: Samuel Paul, Public Affairs Centre, Bangalore, presentation at 6th Global Forum on "Reinventing Governments."
Note: BMP = Bangalore Municipal Corporation; BESCOM = electricity; BWSSB = water supply; BSNL = telecommunications department; BDA = land development authority; BMTC = metropolitan transport coRPORATION; RTO = motor vehicle licensing.

and repeating the report card survey in 1999 and 2003. Figure 4.3 highlights the extraordinary turnaround in perceptions of the quality of service delivery. The Public Affairs Center describes how this was achieved:[83]

> *The first and second report cards had put the city's public agencies under the scanner. The adverse publicity they received, according to many observers, acted as a trigger for corrective action. Inter-agency comparisons seem to have acted as a proxy for competition. Citizen activism and dialogues with the agencies also increased during this early period. These developments prepared the ground for a positive response from the Government. A good example is the political leadership and vision displayed by the Chief Minister S. M. Krishna in the past four years. He provided the framework within which a set of able administrators could set in motion a series of actions and reforms in the agencies. Many civil society groups and the media have stimulated and supported this momentum. Sustaining this movement is the challenge for the future.*

The service provision score card approach pioneered in Bangalore has been widely implemented in countries ranging from Brazil to the Philippines, Ukraine, and Turkey.

A second example involves more hands-on citizen monitoring of official mechanisms and reports of how public resources are used. A few instances are summarized below:

- In Rajasthan, India, building on the passage of a Right to Information Act in the state in 2001, the Movement for the Rights of Peasants and Workers (MKSS) organized public hearings in rural areas, at which figures from the records of licensed distributors of subsidized food rations were compared with figures from the ration books of recipients. Social audits of hospitals were also carried out, during which data from medical records were compared with patients' actual experience. In both cases, large discrepancies between the two sets of figures were revealed. This led to further investigation, which in turn disclosed evidence of corruption, embezzlement, and maladministration.[84]
- A Philippines CSO, the Ateneo University Group, set up a citizen monitoring effort, together with government agencies responsible for textbook distribution and highway infrastructure, to make delivery more effective. The project determined that 21 percent of textbooks were not actually delivered to schools designated to receive them, creating losses of more than US$3 million, which the Department of Education promised to rectify. The template developed for this project has been used by many other CSOs.
- In Tanzania, the Rural Initiatives and Relief Agency helped 10 local communities track government program expenditures for health and education. The pilot projects appear to have helped ensure that commitments to deliver funds were indeed followed through. The expenditure-tracking tool has been made available to CSOs in other rural areas of the country.

The latter two instances were funded by the Partnership for Transparency, an international NGO (supported by Sweden, the UNDP, and the World Bank) that provides micro-grants to CSOs engaged in fighting corruption. Independent evaluations have shown the large majority of these projects to be successful. The maximum grant size provided by the Partnership for Transparency is US$25,000—underscoring that empowerment through information can be a low-cost and high-return strategy for improving governance.

Community-based approaches to local infrastructure investments. In recent years, community-based approaches to local investments have been pursued aggressively under the rubric of community-driven development (CDD). CDD is an approach that "gives control over planning decisions and investment support to community groups and local governments."[85] It seeks to synthesize two types of development interventions that historically have been considered separately from each other—decentralization (discussed in chapter 3), and social investment funds. The latter have been used extensively by donors to transfer resources to poor communities in a participatory way. Between 1999 and 2005, the World Bank alone channeled over US$10 billion to poor communities. According to most reviews, especially in weaker governance settings these CDD operations have been effective in getting services to citizens more cost-effectively and equitably, and have supported participation and accountability. However, fierce debate surrounds the impact of CDD on governance reform more broadly. Underlying this debate are contrasting views regarding the likely interplay, in weaker governance settings, between bottom-up approaches and efforts to strengthen national governance systems.

Certainly, from a governance perspective, the risks are large. As with many donor-funded initiatives, early generation social funds bypassed the public administration with the usual pernicious effects of parallel implementation (see box 4.2). In addition, such programs offer a sometimes-irresistible opportunity to political leaders. In Peru, for example, between 1994 and 2000, over US$900 million was allocated to the Peruvian Social Fund, FONCODES. The poverty benefits were significant: 80 percent of the resources went to the poorest 40 percent of municipalities. Increasingly, however, it became apparent that FONCODES was being used as a source of patronage and popularity by the country's populist president, Alberto Fujimori. Disbursements increased in the months directly preceding elections, and while poorer areas were more likely to get funding, those poorer areas that were "swing voters" were favored in resource allocation.[86]

Learning from experiences such as Peru's, practitioners of CDD have worked to design and implement programs as part of a broader strategy of governance improvement—combining scaled-up participatory resource transfers to communities and longer-run institutional reform—by working closely with line ministries and local governments to help build their capabilities and interactions with community groups. Advocates argue that, especially in weaker governance settings, this hybrid approach can be a powerful way of supporting decentralization. Efforts along these lines are underway in many countries, ranging from Afghanistan to Albania, Brazil, Indonesia, the Kyrgyz Republic, Tanzania, and Zambia. Indonesia and Albania—and, strikingly, Peru post-Fujimori—offer some positive examples of how this integration can proceed (see box 4.4).

But in many other countries where the sponsors of social funds worked hard to try and build an evolutionary bridge to a more sustainable national governance system, they nonetheless failed to evolve much beyond parallel mechanisms. Instead, by seeking to break out of the comfort zone provided by parallel projects, they have brought to the surface the many rivalries and unresolved tensions that characterize countries stuck in a syndrome of weak governance. These include:

- A failure of the intergovernmental rules of the game to evolve in a direction supporting the incremental empowerment of local governments. "Benin, Nepal and Vietnam country studies found that relations between different layers of government remain difficult. Capacity at the lower levels continues to be weak, and the roles of officials at various levels are not clearly defined."[87]
- "Interdepartmental coordination problems (which) arise primarily because government ministries continue to be organized sectorally, and the sectoral culture is so firmly ingrained that it is difficult for departments to work together...for example, in Egypt government staff believed that interdepartmental co-ordination at the higher levels had improved...but co-ordination problems among government staff at the community level persist."[88]
- Competition and tension among implementing NGOs, and sometimes tension at the interface between communities, the agency responsible for CDD-style investments, and local governments.

Surfacing the reality of the difficulty and unpredictability of change in weaker governance settings need not, however, be a bad thing. The challenge for CDD practitioners is to learn more about how to improve the odds: What approaches make success in incrementally fostering sustainable institutional change more likely, and in which country settings? When might the net benefits of a CDD intervention be positive, even with no success in catalyzing institutional change? Demand-driven and incremental institutional reforms, such as CDD, tend to be judged against a standard of perfection. Unsurprisingly, they fall short. What is needed is some agreement as to what *incremental* improvement would look like—and a monitoring approach that systematically tracks and assesses incremental, demand-driven institutional change.

Governance Reform as a Cumulative Process

Chapters 2 and 3 examined some ways in which top-down efforts can, over the long term, improve both bureaucratic effectiveness and oversight by checks-and-balances institutions (including via formal arrangements for participation of citizens at all levels of government). This chapter has explored how more focused, front-line approaches can achieve specific results quite quickly. As the chapter has noted, top-down and front-line approaches often are perceived to be at odds with each

---

BOX 4.4   Linking Community-Based Resource Transfers and Decentralization in Albania, Indonesia, and Peru

Albania. The Albania Development Fund was created in 1993 as a wholly "parallel" mechanism for making participatory resource transfers to communities. Over the subsequent decade it received US$79 million from donors, most of which has gone to the rehabilitation of roads, water supply systems, and schools in rural areas. Communities participate in development activities by identifying local needs. Village councils meet to establish a list of the top three priorities for microprojects, which are then presented to the commune council for consideration, along with the priorities of other villages. The ADF was restructured in 1999, in part to align it more closely with the country's decision to incorporate the key principles of the European Charter of Local Self-Government into its new constitution. Since then, Albania's local (commune) governments have played an increasingly central role in ADF-funded public investments. Commune councils, which are composed of elected village council representatives, select the top three microproject priorities for the entire commune from the village submissions. These priorities are presented to the qark (regional) council as a way to coordinate development between the commune and the regional level. The ADF also has built strong working relationships with sectoral line ministries, including mechanisms that ensure that supported investments are consistent with sectoral master plans. Communes are taking on an increasingly central role in both procurement and implementation (with the ADF serving as guarantor of the competitiveness and transparency of the process). Local governments select and contract for design, construction, and related procurements. Contracting takes place through a competitive bidding process held at ADF headquarters in Tirana. ADF supervises the process as a way to ensure against collusion and other unfair bidding practices, which have posed problems in the past. Maintenance is the responsibility of local governments, and ADF is working with them to build their capacity to take this on.

(continued)

BOX 4.4   Linking Community-Based Resource Transfers and Decentralization in Albania, Indonesia, and Peru (continued)

Indonesia. The country's Kecamatan Development Program (KDP) gives communities planning and decision-making power over development resources. The KDP was begun in 1998, in the aftermath of a major financial crisis and political turmoil. Over three phases, close to US$1 billion has passed through the KDP. The program encompasses 28,000 villages—almost 40 percent of Indonesia's total. The first phase funded more than 50,000 infrastructure and economic activities, benefiting some 35 million poor people. The main reason that the Indonesian government chose to launch the KDP in 1997–8 was that traditional methods for disbursing funds through line ministries had failed. The KDP is able to provide quick, high-volume disbursements of development funds from the national level straight down to the local level. KDP channels funds outside the usual government disbursement mechanisms, allowing financing to flow directly from the national level to kecamatan and village level bank accounts controlled by communities. The direct financing mechanism clears up decision-making bottlenecks caused by central efforts to plan and control activities. KDP's disbursement system takes an average of two weeks between the time when a village places a request and when funds arrive in the village account. Field studies and audits show that KDP projects deliver a broader range of services at lower-than-normal costs, with greater community involvement. Since 1998, Indonesia has progressively systematized its formal system of decentralization. Consequently, the second and third phases of KDP have emphasized greater oversight from district parliaments, government monitoring, links with sectoral agencies such as education and health, district matching grants, and local involvement in drafting formal decentralization regulations on village autonomy. The KDP platform has also provided lessons that are being incorporated into local governance reforms to support greater transparency and participation in district policies related to information disclosure, procurement, budget planning and allocation, leading to higher pro-poor expenditures.

Peru. In Peru, despite FONCODES' close identification with the Fujimori regime, public recognition of it as an effective delivery agency prompted the successor Toledo administration to reform it, rather than shut it down. The reform followed a dual track. First, policy autonomy was eliminated by (i) putting FONCODES as an executing unit under the authority of the newly created Ministry of Women and Social Development (MIMDES), and (ii) transforming FONCODES into an implementation agency that is subcontracted by sector line ministries to carry out investment projects according to rules defined by those ministries. Two recent bank operations (in rural education, and rural water and sanitation) have contributed to cement this new type of arrangement.[89] Second, since 2003 the government has been transforming FONCODES into a conditional fiscal transfer to district governments for social and productive infrastructure. By the end of 2005, 384 of the 1,578 district governments had been accredited to manage FONCODES transfers. Conditions included the formulation of participatory municipal development plans, fulfillment of fiscal transparency regulations, functioning local investment offices, etc. Both FONCODES and the National Decentralization Council provide technical assistance and training to meet those conditions.[89]

Sources: World Bank documents; Wong and Guggenheim 2005.

other. A contrasting perspective, illustrated in figure 4.4, is that their relationship might be mutually reinforcing.

As the figure suggests, better performance of cross-cutting central governance agencies can help front-line performance. In practice, though, as described in chapters 2 and 3, the track record of stand-alone top-down efforts to improve public finance and administrative management is mixed. Top-down initiatives often are not underpinned by a change in the incentives of political and bureaucratic leaders. They are upstream, without well-defined front-line actors (firms, citizens, CSOs, service users, and so forth) to push for results. Especially in weaker governance settings, where expectations and top-down pressures for improved performance may be limited, engaging at the front line has the potential to alter this equation:

- Partial approaches to improve service provision can have positive demonstration effects, with the potential to spur change more broadly.
- Partial (for example, export-focused) reforms of the investment climate can help crowd-in new private firms with the incentive and clout to push for continuing improvements.
- Approaches that enhance transparency and participation empower users of services (citizens, firms, and communities) to press for better public performance.

Heightened pressure on front-line managers to perform has the potential to focus their attention not only on those aspects of service delivery that are under their control, but also on broader systemic constraints that block their ability to perform—such as shortfalls of fiscal resources (including resources that may have been allocated to them), and rigidities in cross-cutting personnel and financial control systems, which prevent well-performing providers from being rewarded, poorly performing providers from being sanctioned, and in general make it frustratingly difficult to get the green light to do anything worthwhile. Increased pressure at the service delivery front line sometimes may thus be transferred upstream, spreading the impulse for reform across the public management system more broadly.

Viewing chapters 2 through 4 as a whole, then, the implied strategy of governance reform can be described as one of "orchestrated imbalance." *Imbalance* is key as a way of building momentum for governance reform by embracing entry

FIGURE 4.4   *A Governance Virtuous Spiral?*

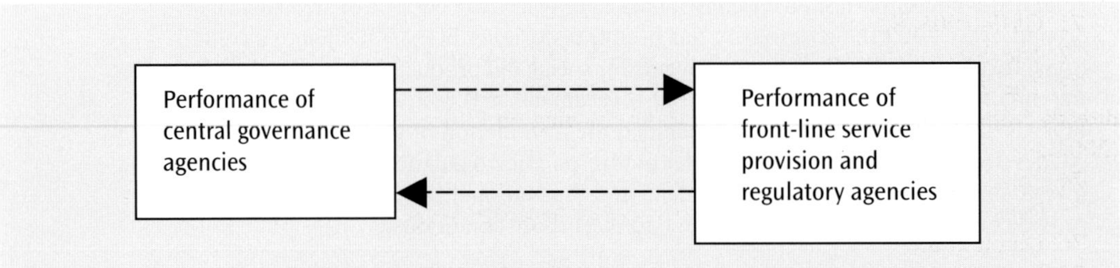

Source: Author.

points for reform that have development impact in the short term, and also ratchet up pressure for reform within the governance system. *Orchestration* is key to assure that binding supply-side public management constraints are addressed before they short-circuit the entire change process. For the latter, it is important that the public management agenda not be defined in so comprehensive a way as to render it unworkable, or incapable of adapting to signals as to what are the emerging "choke points" of change. Throughout, monitoring is crucial—to assure progress on the immediate governance agenda, and to uncover the next round of binding constraints.

Viewed from the perspective of systemic, top-down approaches, conceiving governance and investment climate reform as part of a cumulative process is messy and unpredictable. But, for all that they have not often been part of the discourse on governance reform, such roundabout approaches to change have a venerable pedigree in development economics, notably in debates over "unbalanced" versus "balanced" growth (which were resolved decisively in favor of the former with the triumph of market-driven over more planned approaches to development). Albert Hirschman, one of the giants of development thought over the past half century, put it this way:

> ...*The fundamental problem of development consists in generating and energizing human action in a certain direction...In general, the aim of development policy must be the judicious setting up of sequences and repercussions...to keep alive rather than to eliminate disequilibria...[With this point of departure], advisers would be far less given to determining priorities from the outside...Instead of laying down "first things first" rules, they would try to understand how progress can at times meander strangely through many peripheral areas before it is able to dislodge backwardness from the central positions where it may be strongly entrenched.*[90]

Notes

66. For the detailed analysis on which this subsection is based, see International Monetary Fund and the World Bank (2005).

67. Hausmann, Rodrik, and Velasco (2006) lays out the approach discussed below.

68. For an econometric analysis of this relationship, see Kaufmann and Kraay (2005).

69. For a detailed discussion of road sector reform, see Heggie and Vickers (1998).

70. For a review of the role of community schools in francophone Africa, and the relevant lessons from international experience, see Gershberg and Winkler (2004).

71. GMR 2005, 82–85.

72. The discussion of Export Processing Zones is from World Bank (2005b), 167.

73. The discussion of executive agencies in Tanzania and the United Kingdom is taken directly from Stevens and Teggemann (2004), drawing on Office of Public Service Reform (2002).

74. Pollitt and Bouckaert 2000, 185–86.

75. Details of Thailand's experience are from two papers by Geoffrey Dixon (2002, 2005).

76. Dixon 2005.

77. Kessides, 2004, 3–4, 6.

78. For an early empirical assessment of this tension, see Levy and Spiller, eds. (1996).
79. Kessides 2004, 106–7.
80. Ibid, 8, 17, 18.
81. WDR 2004, 87, 89.
82. Paul 2002, 71.
83. Paul 2002, 71.
84. For information on the MKSS, visit http://www.freedominfo.org/ or contact the organization at mkssrajasthan@yahoo.com. Press coverage of MKSS activities has been extensive and includes Deccan Herald (September 21, 2003) and Mail & Guardian Newspaper, South Africa (February 20, 2004).
85. See http://www.worldbank.org/cdd.
86. Schady 2000.
87. World Bank 2005c, 30.
88. Ibid, 31.
89. See World Bank 2005d.
90. Hirschman 1958, 25, 66, 209.

References

Adserà, Alícia, Carlos Boix, and Mark Payne. 2003. "Are You Being Served? Political Accountability and Governmental Performance." *Journal of Law, Economics, and Organization* 19 (October): 445–90.

Alesina, Alberto; Sule Ozler, Nouriel Roubini and Philip Swagel. 1996. "Political Instability and Economic Growth." *Journal of Economic Growth* 1: 189–211.

Anderson, James and Cheryl Gray. 2006. *Anticorruption in Transition 3: Who is Succeeding.... and Why?* (Washington DC: World Bank).

Barkan, Joel, Ladipo Adamolekun, and Yongmei Zhou. 2004. "Emerging Legislatures: Institutions of Horizontal Accountability." In *Building State Capacity in Africa,* ed. Brian Levy and Sahr Kpundeh. Washington, DC: World Bank Institute.

Barro, Robert. 1991. "Economic Growth in a Cross Section of Countries." *Quarterly Journal of Economics* 106: 407–33.

Bellver, Ana, and Daniel Kaufmann. 2005. "Transparenting Transparency." Mimeo, World Bank, Washington, DC, September. Available at www.worldbank.org/wbi/ governance/wp-transparency.html.

Besley, Timothy, and Robin Burgess. 2002. "The Political Economy of Government Responsiveness: Theory and Evidence from India." *Quarterly Journal of Economics* 117 (4): 1415–51.

Bhatia, Bhavna, and Mohinda Gulati. 2004. "Public Policy for the Power Sector." World Bank Power Sector Note 272, Washington, DC.

Bratton, Michael, and Dominique Van Der Walle. 1998. Democratic Experiments in Africa. New York: Cambridge University Press.

Carothers, Thomas. 2002. "The End of the Transition Paradigm." *Journal of Democracy* 13(1): 5–21.

Carothers, Thomas. 1999. Aiding Democracy Abroad. Washington, DC: Carnegie Endowment for International Peace.

Center for Public Integrity. 2004. "Global Integrity Methodology." Memo, Center for Public Integrity, Washington, DC. Available at www.publicintegrity.org/ga.

Chong, Alberto, and Cesar Calderon 2000. "On the Causality and Feedback Between Institutional Measures and Economic Growth." *Economics and Politics* 12(1): 69–81.

DFID (U.K. Department for International Development). 2005. A Platform Approach to Improving Public Financial Management. Available at www.dfid.gov.uk/aboutdfid/organisation/pfma/pfma-briefing-platform.pdf.

Di Tella, Rafael, and Ernesto Schargrodsky. 2003. "The Role of Wages and Auditing during a Crackdown on Corruption in the City of Buenos Aires." *Journal of Law and Economics* 46 (1): 595–619.

Dixon, Geoffrey. 2002. "Thailand's Hurdle Approach to Budget Reform," World Bank PREM Note Number 73.

Dixon, Geoffrey. 2005. "Thailand's Quest for Results-focused budgeting." *Journal of Public Administration,* 28.

Dorotinsky, Bill, Greg Kisunko, and Shilpa Pradhan. 2005. "Public Expenditure Management System Performance in Heavily Indebted Countries, 2002–2004." PREM Note, World Bank, Washington, DC.

Economic and Social Research Foundation. 2005. "Enhancing Aid Relationships in Tanzania: Independent Monitoring Group 2005." Dar Es Salaam.

Engberg-Pedersen, Poul and Brian Levy, 2004. "Building State Capacity in Africa: Learning from Performance and Results," in Levy and Kpundeh (eds.), *Building State Capacity in Africa.*

Gelb, Alan, and Benn Eifert. 2005. "Improving the Dynamics of Aid: Toward More Predictable Budget Support." Policy Research Working Paper 3732, World Bank, Washington, DC.

Gelb, Alan, Brian Ngo, and Xiao Ye. 2004. "Implementing Performance-Based Aid in Africa: The Country Policy and Institutional Assessment." World Bank Africa Region Working Paper Series, #77, November.

Gershberg, Alec, and Don Winkler. 2004. "Education Decentralization in Africa: A Review of Recent Policy and Practice." In *Building State Capacity in Africa,* ed. Brian Levy and Sahr Kpundeh. Washington, DC: World Bank Institute.

Gray, Cheryl, Joel Hellman, and Randi Ryterman. 2004. *Anticorruption in Transition 2: Corruption in Enterprise-State Interactions in Europe and Central Asia, 1999–2002.* Washington DC: World Bank.

Grindle, Merilee. 2004. "Good Enough Governance: Poverty Reduction and Reform in Developing Countries." *Governance* 17(4) (October): 525–48.

Hager, Barry M. 2000. "The Rule of Law: A Lexicon for Policy Makers." The Mansfield Center for Pacific Affairs. www.mansfielddn.org/programs/program_pdfs/lexicon.pdf.

Hausmann, Ricardo, Dani Rodrik, and Andres Velasco. 2006. "Getting the diagnosis Right: A New Approach to Economic Reform," *Finance and Development* (March): 13.

Heggie, Ian, and Piers Vickers. 1998. "Commercial Management and Financing of Roads." Technical Paper 409, World Bank, Washington, DC.

Heidenhof, Guenter, Helene Grandvoinnet, Daryoush Kianpour, and Bobak Rezaian. 2002. "Design and Implementation of Financial Management Systems: An African Perspective." Africa Region Working Paper Series 25, World Bank, Washington, DC.

Hirschman, Albert O. 1958. *The Strategy of Economic Development.* New Haven: Yale University Press.

IDA (International Development Association). 2004. "Measuring Results: Improving National Statistics in IDA Countries." Washington, DC. siteresources. worldbank.org/IDA/ Resources/MeasuringResultsStatistics.pdf.

IDA (International Development Association) and IMF (International Monetary Fund). 2005. "Update on the Assessments and Implementation of Action Plans to Strengthen Capacity of HIPCs to Track Poverty-Reducing Public Spending." Washington, DC. www.imf.org/ external/np/pp/eng/2005/041205a.pdf.

IMF (International Monetary Fund), Fiscal Affairs Department. 2005. IMF Technical Assistance Evaluation: Public Expenditure Management Reform in Anglophone African Countries, Washington, DC, August.

International Monetary Fund and the World Bank. 2005. "Fiscal Policy for Growth and Development: An Interim Report for the Development Committee," April 2005.

Islam, Roumeen, ed. 2002. *The Right to Tell: The Role of Mass Media in Economic Development.* Washington, DC: World Bank Institute Development Studies.

Kaufmann, Daniel, Aart Kraay, and Massimo Mastruzzi. 2005. "Governance Matters IV: Governance Indicators for 1996–2004." Policy Research Paper 3630, World Bank, Washington, DC.

Kaufmann, Daniel, Aart Kraay, and Pablo Zoido-Lobaton. 1999. "Governance Matters." World Bank Policy Research Paper Series, # 2196.

Keefer, Philip E. 2005. "Democratization and clientelism: Why are Young Democracies Badly Governed?" *World Bank Policy Research Working Paper* 3594, May.

Keefer, Philip E., and Stuti Khemani. 2005. "Democracy, Public Expenditures and the Poor," *World Bank Research Observer* (Spring): 1–27.

Kessides, Ioannis. 2004. *Reforming Infrastructure: Privatization, Regulation and Competition.* Washington, DC: World Bank and Oxford University Press.

Khan, Mushtaq H. 2002. "State Failure in Developing Countries and Strategies of Institutional Reform." Draft paper for ABCDE conference, Oslo, June 24–26.

Kiragu, Kithinji Rwekaza Mukandala, and Denyse Morin. 2004. "Reforming Pay Policy: Techniques, Sequencing, and Politics," in Levy and Kpundeh (eds.), *Building State Capacity in Africa.*

Knack, Stephen and Philip Keefer. 1995. "Institutions and Economic Performance: Cross-Country Tests Using Alternative Institutional Measures." *Economics and Politics* 7: 207–27.

Levy, Brian, and Pablo Spiller, eds. 1996. *Regulations, Institutions, and Commitment.* New York: Cambridge University Press.

Levy, Brian, and Sahr Kpundeh, eds. 2004. *Building State Capacity in Africa.* Washington, DC: World Bank Institute.

Lewis, Peter M. 1996. "Economic Reform and Political Transition in Africa: The Quest for a Politics of Development." *World Politics* 49(1): 92–129.

Marshall, Monty, and Keith Jaggers. 2002. "POLITY IV Project: Political Regime Characteristics and Transitions, 1800–2002." Dataset Users' Manual, Center for International Development and Conflict Management, University of Maryland.

Mauro, Paolo. 1998. "Corruption and Growth." *Quarterly Journal of Economics* 110: 681–712.

Mendel, Toby. 2004. *Freedom of Information: A Comparative Legal Survey.* New Delhi, India: United Nations Educational, Scientific and Cultural Organization.

Migdal, Joel. 1988. *Strong Societies and Weak States.* Princeton, N.J.: Princeton University Press.

North, Douglass. 1990. *Institutions, Institutional Change, and Economic Performance.* New York: Cambridge University Press.

OAS (Organization of American States). 2003. "Annual Report of the Special Rapporteur for Freedom of Expression 2003."

Office of Public Service Reform. 2002. *Better Government Service: Executive Agencies in the 21st Century.* London: The Stationery Office.

Olson, Mancur. 1991. *The Logic of Collective Action.* Cambridge, Mass.: Harvard University Press.

Paul, Samuel. 2002. *Holding the State to Account: Citizen Monitoring in Action.* Bangalore, India: Books for Change.

PEFA (Public Expenditure and Financial Accountability Secretariat). 2005. "Public Financial Management Performance Measurement Framework." Washington, DC.

Pollitt, C., and Bouckaert, G. 2000. *Public Management Reform: A Comparative Analysis.* Oxford, U.K.: Oxford University Press.

Rajkumar, Andrew, and Vinaya Swaroop. 2002. "Public Spending and Outcomes: Does Governance Matter?" World Bank Policy Working Paper 2840, Washington, DC.

Rigo, A., and H. J. Gruss. 1991. "The Rule of Law." Background paper for the Task Force on Governance, World Bank, Washington, DC.

Sage, Caroline, and Michael Woolcock. 2005. "Breaking Legal Inequality Traps: New Approaches to Building Justice Systems for the Poor in Developing Countries." Paper presented at Arusha Conference on New Frontiers of Social Policy.

Schady, Norbert. 2000. "The Political Economy of Expenditures by the Peruvian Social Fund (FONCODES), 1991–1995." *American Political Science Review* 94 (2): 289–303.

Sen, Amartya. 1999. *Development as Freedom.* New York: Random House.

Stephenson, Matthew C. 2005. "Judicial Reform in Developing Countries: Constraints and Opportunities." Harvard Law School, draft, December 2005, 9.

Stevens, Mike and Stefanie Teggemann 2004. "Comparative Experience with Public Service Sector Reform in Ghana, Tanzania, and Zambia." In *Building State Capacity in Africa,* ed. Levy and Kpundeheds. Washington, DC: World Bank.

Strömberg, David. 2004. "Radio's Impact on Public Spending." *Quarterly Journal of Economics* 119 (1): 189–221.

Svensson, Jakob. 2005. "Eight Questions about Corruption." *Journal of Economic Perspectives* 19 (3): 19–42.

Swaroop, Vinaya, and Andrew Sunil Rajkumar. 2002. "Public Spending and Outcomes: Does Governance Matter?" Policy Research Working Paper 2840, World Bank, Washington, DC.

UNDP (United Nations Development Programme). 2004. *Governance Indicators: A Users Guide.* New York: Bureau for Development Policy, Democratic Governance Group, and European Commission, Eurostat Unit.

White, Roland, and Paul Smoke. 2005. "East Asia Decentralizes." In *East Asia Decentralizes: Making Local Government Work*. Washington, DC: World Bank.

Woolcock, Michael, and Caroline Sage. 2005. "Breaking Legal Inequality Traps: New Approaches to Building Justice Systems for the Poor in Developing Countries." Prepared for Social Development and Policy Conference, December 2005.

Wong, Susan, and Scott Guggenheim. 2005. "Community-Driven Development: Decentralization's Accountability Challenge." In *East Asia Decentralizes: Making Local Government Work*. Washington, DC: World Bank.

World Bank. 2006. *Global Monitoring Report: Strengthening Mutual Accountability, Aid, Trade, and Governance*. Washington, DC: World Bank.

————. 2005a. "Enabling Country Capacity to Achieve Results: 2005 CDF Progress Report." Operations Policy and Country Services, World Bank, Washington, DC.

————. 2005b. *World Development Report: A Better Investment Climate for Everyone*. Washington, DC: World Bank.

————. 2005c. "The Effectiveness of World Bank Support for Community Based and Driven Development." Operations Evaluation Department, Washington DC.

————. 2005d. "Social Safety Nets in Peru: Background Paper for RECURSO."

World Bank and IMF. 2005a. "2005 PRS Review: Balancing Accountabilities and Scaling Up Results." PREM Poverty Reduction Group, World Bank, Washington, DC.

————. 2004a. *World Development Report 2004, Making Services Work for Poor People*. Washington, DC: Oxford University Press for the World Bank.

————. 2004b. "Country Policy and Institutional Assessments: 2004 Assessment Questionnaire." World Bank Operations Policy and Country Services, Washington, DC, December.

————. 1999. Civil Service Reform: A Review of World Bank Assistance. World Bank Operations Evaluation Department. Report number 19599, August 4.

World Bank and EBRD (European Bank for Reconstruction and Development). 1999, 2002, and 2005. Business Environment and Enterprise Surveys. Washington, DC.

Yang, Dean. 2005. "Integrity for Hire: An Analysis of a Widespread Program for Combating Customs Corruption." Gerald R. Ford School of Public Policy, University of Michigan, Ann Arbor Working Paper Series, Number 2005–001.

Appendix:
Applying the Indicators—
A Typology of Countries

(prepared jointly with Ceren Ozer)

This appendix examines, for 62 low-income aid recipient countries,[91] the relationships among six of the core governance indicators highlighted in this study. Between them, the six measures address the three main elements of governance framework—bureaucratic quality, quality of checks-and-balances institutions, and corruption, one performance outcomes of the governance system.

Figure A-1 and table A-1 organize the countries into five distinct groups according to the relative strengths and weaknesses of bureaucratic quality and the quality of checks-and-balances institutions. The countries are grouped via a four-step process:

1. Standardizing each of the five subsystem measures—public financial management (CPIA13); quality of public administration (CPIA 15); voice and accountability (Kaufmann-Kraay); rule of law (Kaufmann-Kraay), also CPIA12); executive constraints (Polity IV)—on a common distribution. Each measure is linearly transformed to range between minimum -1 and maximum 1;
2. Grouping the measures into the two key dimensions (bureaucratic quality and the quality of checks-and-balances institutions) and calculating average scores for each. The bureaucratic quality measure is the average of linearly transformed CPIA 13 and CPIA 15. The checks-and-balances measure is the average of linearly transformed Kaufmann Kraay's (KK) voice and accountability and rule of law, and the Polity IV database executive constraints measures;
3. Grouping countries into higher-, middling- and lower-governance performers based on the sum of the scores (maximum 1.34; minimum -1.514; average 0.008; median 0.129) for the two dimensions; and
4. Within the middling group, using the difference (maximum 0.673; minimum -1.369; average -.079; median -0.133) between the two scores to distinguish among three subgroups.

FIGURE A.1   IDA Countries Grouped by Bureaucratic Quality and Checks and Balance

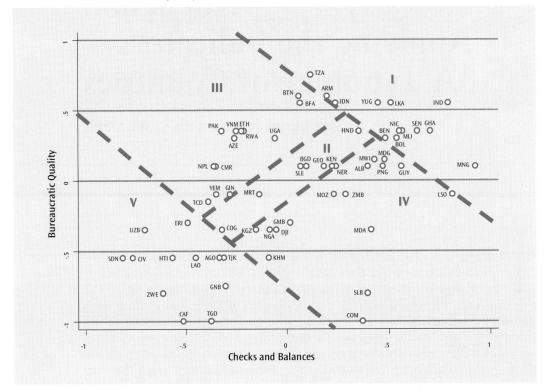

Source: Author.

The five groups in the figure and the table comprise the following:

- 13 countries with better overall governance performance; (Group I)
- 37 countries with middling governance performance, of which
  - 8 countries have middling performance on both dimensions (II)
  - 13 countries are stronger on bureaucratic quality than on checks and balances (III)
  - 16 countries are stronger on checks and balances than bureaucratic quality (IV)
- 12 countries with weaker governance performance (Group V)

Using ordinary least squares regression, it is possible to examine in a preliminary way the relationship between the quality of institutions (measured by the five variables highlighted above) and governance outcomes (measured by the quality of policies and control over corruption). The regression results can be used to provide some insight in the effectiveness of a country's control over corruption.

The fourth column of table A-1 breaks down the 62 IDA-eligible country sample into three broad groups with respect to their KK control of corruption score—

"top" being the top third of performers among the 62 country sample. On the assumption that control of corruption is, in part, dependent on the quality of underlying institutions, it is interesting to compare the actual level of control of corruption with its predicted value from an OLS regression, using the KK control of corruption as the dependent variable and the 5 subsystem indicators as the right hand-side variables. The last column of table A-1 reports the difference between the actual score and the predicted score. "Better" means that actual level of control of corruption is better than the predicted level; "middle" stands for a good fit; and "worse" means that given the level of governance subsystem indicators, we would expect the country to have performed better in controlling corruption.

TABLE A.1 IDA Countries Grouped by Bureaucratic Quality and Checks and Balances with Level of Actual and Predicted Corruption

Better overall governance (high sum)				
	Sum	Difference	KK Control of Corruption	Actual control of corruption relative to predicted
Balanced				
India	1.340	-0.240	Top	Middle
Sri Lanka	1.058	0.042	Top	Better
Serbia and Montenegro	0.997	0.103	Top	Better
Stronger Checks and Balance				
Ghana	1.053	-0.353	Top	Better
Mongolia	1.026	-0.826	Top	Worse
Senegal	0.988	-0.288	Top	Middle
Bolivia	0.915	-0.215	Middle	Worse
Nicaragua	0.900	-0.200	Top	Better
Mali	0.837	-0.237	Top	Middle
Benin	0.781	-0.181	Top	Better
Stronger Bureaucratic Quality				
Tanzania	0.866	0.634	Top	Middle
Armenia	0.797	0.403	Top	Middle
Indonesia	0.789	0.311	Middle	Middle

Middling overall governance-stronger on checks and balances				
	Sum	Difference	KK Control of Corruption	Actual control of corruption relative to predicted
High Middling				
Lesotho	0.713	-0.913	Top	Better
Guyana	0.661	-0.461	Top	Better
Madagascar	0.628	-0.328	Top	Better
Malawi	0.580	-0.280	Middle	Worse
Papua New Guinea	0.571	-0.371	Middle	Middle
Albania	0.497	-0.297	Middle	Middle

(continued)

TABLE A.1 IDA Countries Grouped by Bureaucratic Quality and Checks and Balances with Level of Actual and Predicted Corruption (continued)

	Sum	Difference	KK Control of Corruption	Actual control of corruption relative to predicted
Middling				
Zambia	0.188	-0.388	Middle	Worse
Mozambique	0.132	-0.332	Middle	Worse
Moldova	0.063	-0.763	Middle	Middle
Low-middling				
Gambia, The	-0.285	-0.315	Middle	Worse
Djibouti	-0.403	-0.297	Middle	Worse
Solomon Islands	-0.405	-1.195	Bottom	Middle
Nigeria	-0.436	-0.264	Bottom	Better
Kyrgyz Republic	-0.504	-0.196	Middle	Better
Comoros	-0.631	-1.369	Bottom	Middle
Cambodia	-0.640	-0.460	Middle	Middle

Middling governance-balanced

	Sum	Difference	KK Control of Corruption	Actual control of corruption relative to predicted
High-middling				
Honduras	0.702	-0.002	Middle	Worse
Kenya	0.342	-0.142	Middle	Middle
Niger	0.324	-0.124	Middle	Middle
Georgia	0.283	-0.083	Middle	Middle
Bangladesh	0.196	0.004	Bottom	Worse
Sierra Leone	0.168	0.032	Middle	Middle
Low-middling				
Mauritania	-0.236	0.036	Top	Better
Congo, Rep. of	-0.671	-0.029	Bottom	Middle

Middling overall governance-stronger on bureaucratic quality

	Sum	Difference	KK Control of Corruption	Actual control of corruption relative to predicted
High-middling				
Bhutan	0.659	0.541	Top	Better
Burkina Faso	0.615	0.485	Top	Better
Middling				
Uganda	0.242	0.358	Middle	Middle
Rwanda	0.139	0.561	Top	Better
Vietnam	0.126	0.574	Middle	Middle
Ethiopia	0.101	0.599	Middle	Middle
Azerbaijan	0.041	0.559	Bottom	Worse
Pakistan	0.027	0.673	Middle	Worse

(continued)

TABLE A.1 IDA Countries Grouped by Bureaucratic Quality and Checks and Balances with Level of Actual and Predicted Corruption (continued)

	Sum	Difference	KK Control of Corruption	Actual control of corruption relative to predicted
Low-middling				
Nepal	-0.252	0.452	Middle	Middle
Cameroon	-0.263	0.463	Middle	Middle
Guinea	-0.382	0.182	Middle	Middle
Yemen, Republic of	-0.450	0.250	Middle	Middle
Chad	-0.539	0.239	Bottom	Worse

Low overall governance (low sum)				
	Sum	Difference	KK Control of Corruption	Actual control of corruption relative to predicted
Eritrea	-0.791	0.191	Middle	Better
Tajikistan	-0.861	-0.239	Bottom	Middle
Angola	-0.885	-0.215	Bottom	Middle
Lao PDR	-1.002	-0.098	Bottom	Middle
Guinea-Bissau	-1.054	-0.446	Middle	Better
Uzbekistan	-1.055	0.355	Bottom	Middle
Haiti	-1.119	0.019	Bottom	Worse
Côte d'Ivoire	-1.315	0.215	Bottom	Middle
Sudan	-1.366	0.266	Bottom	Middle
Togo	-1.376	-0.624	Middle	Middle
Zimbabwe	-1.416	-0.184	Bottom	Better
Central African Republic.	-1.514	-0.486	Bottom	Worse

Source: Author.

Notes

91. The 66 countries identified in the main body of the paper, less four countries for which the Polity IV executive constraints measures are not available—Bosnia and Herzegovina, Burundi, the Democratic Republic of Congo, and São Tomé and Principe.

Index

A

A Better Investment Climate for Everyone,
    91–92
accountability, 4, 6, 6f, 108–110, xx, xxi,
    xxxi–xxxii, xxxivt
  and transparency, 71, 72f
  decentralization effects, 65
  effects of adverse publicity, 107
  for development effectiveness, 90
  improving from front line, 100
  information use, 106
  KK, 80, 80t
  media role, 78
  mutual, 9–10, 50, xix
  quality of checks-and-balances insti-
      tutions, 82t
  top-down, 100–105
accountability groups, 59, 60b
accounting, 33, 33f, 53t, xxiii
actionable indicators, 10–11, 23, 24, xxvii
  budget quality, 35
  checks-and-balances institutions, 58
  public administrative quality, 44b
  rule of law and justice, 69
  actors, 6f, xx
Africa Capacity Building Foundation
      (ACBF), 76–77
African Development Bank, 14b, 15b
African Economic Research Consortium
      (AERC), 76
aggregate indicators, 19b

aggregation approach, 15–16
aid, 48–50, xxxvi
    allocation, 33, xxxvi
Albania, 44b, 48, 49t
Albanian Development Fund, 110b
American Reinventing Government Initia-
      tive, 100
Andhra Pradesh, India, electricity reform,
      94b
Ateneo University Group, 108
audits, PEFA indicators, 53t

B

Bangladesh, 95, 96t, 97t, xxxii, xxxt
Baseline Indicator Set (BIS), 23, 39b
Benin, 64b
binding constraints approach, 92–93
Bolivia, 39
bottom-up accountability, 105–110, xxxii
Brazil, budget oversight, 60
bribery, 20f
budget cycle, 33, 33f, xxiii, xxivf
    PEFA indicators, 53t
budget implementation, patterns, 36, 36t
budget management, 37, 40, 41, 43, 45
    by HIPC, 36t
    correlations, 47t
    CPIA, 51t–52t
    overall quality patterns, 34
    prioritizing investments, 91
    quality assessments, xxiv

ECO-AUDIT
Environmental Benefits Statement

The World Bank is committed to preserving endangered forests and natural resources. The Office of the Publisher has chosen to print *Governance Reform* on recycled paper with 25 percent post-consumer content in accordance with the recommended standards for paper usage set by the Green Press Initiative, a nonprofit program supporting publishers in using fiber that is not sourced from endangered forests. For more information, visit www.greenpressinitiative.org

Saved:
- 7 trees
- 5 million BTUs of energy
- 821 lbs. of CO_2 greenhouse gases
- 2,692 gallons of wastewater
- 445 lbs. of solid waste